The Day After Jimmy Got Saved

Reflections on Growing Up Mennonite in Knoxville

To honor the memory
of Mr. Charles Shearer
5th grade teacher
Lonsdale Elementary School
Knoxville, Tennessee

You helped me

Afterword

Forward

"Why did you go and do that for? And there you have the problem. Him and Jimmy had done worked out the rules of the cussin' club, and Jimmy went and changed the rules, all on his own, just on account of he got saved the night before. Rules were like that. They applied until they didn't, and then they got changed. Except for a Mennonite boy, the rules were worked out in holy places like Harrisonburg, Virginia or Greenwood, Delaware, and they stayed the same. So, they just had to fit, even when they didn't.

So what was a boy to do? Well, like his mother who sold savings bonds with the PTA while wearing the regulation prayer veiling and cape dress, he adjusted accordingly. He figured it out as he went along. He took up with Jimmy, and maybe some of the rules got bent just a little bit. Most of the time nobody knew, so it didn't matter.

Here is part of the story about the rules and the bending and the good times figuring it all out. I'm sure most of it is almost true. We're brothers, and he told it to me, and I don't lie.

Don Yoder
Pulaski, VA

Introduction

In March 2002, Mennonite Health Assembly met in Knoxville, Tennessee, my hometown. 2002 was the 50th anniversary of Mennonite Health Assembly, and Mennonite historian John Sharp entertained us with stories from the last 50 years of MHA.

Afterwards, I got to thinking about this. If anybody should have been telling stories to a bunch of Mennonites meeting in Knoxville, it should have been me. I grew up there in a rather small Mennonite community, and that experience shaped my life in powerful ways. Anabaptist thought and theology do not mix well with southern culture, and trying to come to grips with that dichotomy as a young boy created many moments for reflection. Growing up in the south is interesting enough in its own right, but adding the ethnic, religious and cultural overtones of being raised as a traditional Mennonite created rather special circumstances for my years in Tennessee.

With John's encouragement, I began to put words to my memories. When an idea would strike, I would work on a story. Some of my friends were entertained with the results. Some members of my extended family liked them. Others had concerns. For me, the process yielded an unexpected result. I discovered that completing a story helped me to appreciate that part of my life in a new way. I wanted to tell the stories because they are _my_ stories, and that has its own compulsion for expression. And the stories kept coming, and coming...

The environment I grew up is mostly a thing of the past, nearly extinct, and nobody will know about it unless I tell it. And another thing. I bet there are lots of people that didn't grow up Mennonite in Knoxville that know a little bit of what it was like, even if the physical or theological landscape was different in their growing up years. And growing up is what most of us had to do, willy-nilly, whether we liked it or not.

So, here are some of the stories. The characters are real and the events are factual. I say that clearly and without a doubt, because this is the way I remember it.

Many names and other identifying information have been altered. That seemed prudent.

As you will note, there is a considerable time gap between 2002 and 2016, when I finally got around to making a book out of these stories. I wasn't all that interested in going public.

It was my little sister who went ahead and printed up a copy for each of the siblings, with a not-too-subtle indication that they would be spread abroad, either by her, or by me. I said, well OK. Maybe I will get around to it. Every once in a while she says, "Ken? How is it coming along?" So, in order to keep peace in the family, here you have it.

Little Sister, if somebody gets all twitchy and everything on account of these stories, it is on you!

Ken Yoder
Quakertown, PA   May 2016

Growing Up Mennonite in Knoxville

It was a challenge to grow up Mennonite in Knoxville in the 1950's and 60's. Mennonites like to be a communal people, and there weren't many Mennonites in Knox County, Tennessee to be communal with. We felt quite isolated and I grew up with a clear sense that the non-Mennonites, of which there were many, were not to be trusted, because they would lead you astray. We were to be a separate people, and needed to be different from the world around us.

And we were. Folks in Tennessee didn't know what to make out of us, the Mennonites, neither did we, as far as that went. We were strange ducks, and felt it, for sure. When my younger sister got baptized and had to wear her covering to school, her classmate said to her one day, "You ain't no minny-night and you know it." Folks in Tennessee didn't get it.

Since there weren't many of us to relate to, and we were sort of suspicious of the intentions of our neighbors, it made growing up Mennonite in Knoxville a bit awkward. I wanted to belong, to fit in somewhere, but "fitting in" in Knoxville was by definition off limits.

Fitting in with Mennos in other locations was difficult, based on geography, theology, and suspicion. Today some may call it paranoia, but back then it was reality - some of those other Mennonites weren't to be trusted either. They knew better and deliberately wanted to lead you astray. They hadn't been raised properly was the general consensus.

If the truth must be known, I kindly wanted to be led astray if I ever got the chance, as long as I could count on getting redeemed in time. And besides, I knew Brother Jennings, and everybody in East Tennessee knew Brother Jennings. He was a good man, a godly man, and I figured that would count for something if push came to shove.

The focus on holy living meant that you couldn't cuss, chew, smoke, drink, attend basketball games, or do

5

anything else that was interesting to me. That tended to limit the scope of activities pretty good.

It also meant that holy things like communion time were kind of scary. A Virginia bishop would come twice a year to Knoxville in a black suit, black hat, black car, and forgive me, they came with sort of a black presence. We would get fixed up for communion. I dreaded those visits a whole lot, even though we were told communion was something to look forward to, something joyous. It wasn't a happy time for me at all, as we would have to attest that we were at peace with God and with our fellow man as far as we knew, and that we were worthy of taking communion. And if we weren't, we had to get ready fast. So, I wound up telling ritual lies twice a year.

The consequence of taking communion unworthily was too dreadful to contemplate. We were given ample opportunity to think about it. A frequent diet of frightful end times sermons, complete with charts and graphic descriptions of the Great Tribulation, coupled with Bible Belt theology of burning in hell-fire forever - well, let's just say that a young boy with a creative imagination had a lot to worry about all by himself.

We had a copy of <u>Martyrs' Mirror</u> and I read in it. The <u>Martyrs' Mirror</u> was a collection of stories about those Anabaptists right in the middle of the Protestant Reformation over there in Switzerland and Germany and about how they got persecuted and killed all over the place because of their faith. Those Catholics and Lutherans and Reformed people didn't like each other very much, and none of them liked the Anabaptists. They wanted to kill the Anabaptists. Just knowing what could happen to us at any time put a damper on frivolity. Being holy meant you needed to look forward to suffering. I knew I was supposed to rejoice in suffering, like those people in <u>Martyrs' Mirror</u>, but in my heart I had problems with that. I didn't want to suffer, but it seemed that was something we were supposed to do, based on history.

It appeared to me that growing up Mennonite in Knoxville should have qualified as fulfilling the suffering required of the faithful, but the cup of sorrow never seemed to get full.

Something had to change so I could move on with the growing up business, and that is what I set out to do, even if it put a dent in the fender of holiness now and again.

Now Jimmy, He Was My Friend

Once in a while good things happen, even when you don't expect it, and it happened to me. I am so glad it happened. It happened when we moved out west of Knoxville, and I started 6th grade at Ball Camp School. There I met Jimmy, rogue, rascal, and true American hero. Jimmy knew all about hell-fire, but it didn't seem to bother him too much. In fact, he was sort of cheerful about it. I decided that Jimmy would make a good friend for me. Jimmy would be the Id to the Superego of being Mennonite in Knoxville.

Jimmy had lots of vices that made him attractive to me. He could cuss with great conviction, creativity, fluency, and breath-taking intensity. He feared neither man nor beast, powers present nor future, temporal nor spiritual. He was all that no proper Mennonite should never be, but he had fun.

"Hey, Jimmy, where you going?" I would ask him. "To hell, if I don't start doing better," would be his response. Hell couldn't be all that bad if Jimmy was planning to be there. The chances of me getting in the other place seemed rather remote based on what I was hearing in church. And besides, if it was supposed to be such a happy place, why did people get all glum and serious when they talked about it? I decided to hedge my bets - I would run with Jimmy and hope for a chance to make a good deathbed confession in case I changed my mind in the end.

Jimmy was disrespectful. The teacher would yell, "Listen! Listen!" Jimmy would call back, "Cat's a-pissin'." Then I would say, "Where at?" And Jimmy would say, "In yo' hat." And the sky didn't fall in contrary to what I was sure would happen.

Jimmy would get grounded by his Momma on a regular basis, but it didn't bother him none. He would sneak away anyhow and we would go fishing. How he could fish! Worm fishing was what we did mostly, although wasper larvae would really attract the brim fish.

9

A big wad of worms on the fish hook was good for the bass over in what Jimmy called "bass hole." And that red and white popper - that was a real good plug until I lost it for Jimmy and he cussed me. Like he did that time we were fishing and I stumbled and dumped the worms down the creek. So we had to go graveling instead, where you go for fish with your hands. Jimmy got some. I saw it with my own eyes.

Jimmy was daring, courting sure destruction. We were up a tree in Mr. Smith's woods one day, and someone started yelling at us. "HEY BOYS, WHAT YE THINK YE DOING UP THAT TREE THERE?" Jimmy yelled right back, "None-a yo' business." I was scared to death that it was Mr. Lee, whom I had never met, but had sure heard about. He was the father of Jason and them, a bum who supposedly lived in a hollowed-out stump up in the woods. "Jimmy," I hissed. "Shut up. You going to make him mad." "HEY BOYS. I'M SERI'US. WHAT'S YE NAMES?" "Ain't a-telling." "I GOT ME A GUN HERE. YOU BETTER TELL ME." "Ain't a-gonna." I heard something snapping, and wailed, "Jimmy. He gonna shoot us. We gotta up and get down out of this tree." And down we went and run like two scared boys, which we were.

Jimmy could turn almost anything into a risqué event. One day Ralph, who for me was the yang to Jimmy's yin, was eating a hot dog in a bun down in the lunchroom. Jimmy already ate his lunch and we were watching Ralph eat his wiener with a fork. Each time Ralph would stab or cut the hot dog, Jimmy would kindly wince and say, "Ouch." Ralph just couldn't figure this out, but since I was already of dubious moral standards, I KNEW what it was about. I also knew that your generic Baptists and other sinners could talk about what was down there, but good Mennonites were supposed to ignore these things. But for me, the specter of an upcoming communion just couldn't compete with the pleasure of guilty glee.

10

Most Mennonites learned a-capella singing in church. I had a head start there. The refining touches came at school. Me and Jimmy and his friends would sit in the lunch room in 6th-7th grade and sing that awesome beer commercial, "Let's get together with a glass of Schlitz," in three part harmony. We never got to drink any of it, however. Jimmy said beer was horse piss, because of the color and the head of foam on it. That took our appetite for beer away.

Jimmy taught me much useful information, by precept and example. We were both poor, so we didn't have money for cigarettes, and we were too proud to pick butts up off the road. But Jimmy knew about rabbit tobacco that grows wild. It can be chewed or smoked. I tried smoking it, but didn't inhale. I had convictions about smoking, and limited most of my rabbit tobacco days to chewing. So Jimmy and me would use rabbit tobacco when our friend Wilson simultaneously smoked a cigarette and a cigar, while chewing Bull of the Woods chewing tobacco. I was quite impressed, especially when Wilson was suddenly indisposed. Rather violently, as I recall. It all started with slobber running out of the corner of his mouth. Didn't end that way.

You know, I suppose with mature reflection I should have some regrets about my friendship. I got to tell you that I don't have one regret at all. Why? I will tell you why. Altogether, Jimmy, he was my friend, a fine friend, and I sure needed one. It was best, however, that I keep my Jimmy life and my other life sort of separate, being as I didn't want too many complications.

The Day After Jimmy Got Saved

For a sure and certain fact, one of Jimmy's finest attributes, one that I made sure was kept hidden, was his ability to cuss. Oh my goodness gracious, how he could cuss, and I was so envious. You can already guess this admiration created a bit of tension for me, as Mennonites in Knoxville didn't cuss. They developed concerns, got hurt and silent. For me, that didn't work real good. It didn't help me feel better, or to deal with the strains of my life.

Now you talk about dealing with things, Jimmy, he had a sure-fire coping mechanism. He could cuss. It was truly wonderful to be in the presence of Jimmy when he would go on a cussing tear. He let it rip real good, and when he was done, there weren't lingering feelings. Not cursing, as your chances of burning in hell-fire forever increased if you took the name of the Lord in vain, or used the big "D" word. And as far as the "F" word was concerned - well. Everybody, including Jimmy, knew it was definitely off limits. That was cursing.

Cussing was something I was not allowed to do at home for sure, neither was Jimmy, but that didn't stop him. His cussing prowess was legendary. Based on my at-home values, I was seriously handicapped in the cussing department, and resented being left behind.

Hence, the formation of the Cussing Club. In private, with Jimmy as the mentor, some of us cussing-challenged boys would meet for regular practice sessions, which had a more positive bonding effect than sitting in the Knoxville church being terrified about the end times, the unpardonable sin, the Russians coming, the Battle of Armageddon, and communion. Lord, how I worked at it, the cussing, that is. I had so much time to make up.

One communion time, I knew I was unworthy, and tried to clear my slate with Jimmy. "I know I ain't been a very good Mennonite," I explained to Jimmy as we ran across a field. That was all I could get out. Didn't make no difference to him - I was OK in his book.

13

That is why I stuck with Jimmy one time when he got grounded. We had a camping trip planned, and he wasn't allowed to ride his bike. However, his momma didn't say anything about him doubling on my bike. Besides, that evening Jimmy either coerced his sister to mow his patch of the lawn or paid her a quarter to do it, I don't know which. All I know is, I rode in his lane, with a big tarp folded up on the basket. Jimmy sallied out and hopped on the cross bar and away we went. Somebody hollered, "JIMMY," real loud like, but that wasn't my name so I kept on peddling hard as I could until we got out of shouting distance.

But the hand of the Lord fell heavily upon Jimmy, as he was struck with diarrhea in a mighty way, and he winced and moaned with each bump. "Hold on to that tarp," I said to Jimmy, "or it will surely fall off." With him being in such awful straights, his mind was not focused like it should have been on the tarp, and it slid down over the front wheel of the bike. "Jimmy!" I said. "YODER," he wept, and we bounced over the tarp. The bump was too much. Jimmy lost his grip and messed his pants. He blamed it on me in is usual colorful fashion, and had to hide in the ditch by the road while he tossed away his soiled underwear. I was secretly amused, and we went on camping anyways.

In a way, it was an honor to be cussed by Jimmy. You knew you were in the presence of greatness in the world of cussing. He had that gift that we all, except for folks like Mennonite bishops from Virginia, aspire to but seldom achieve. I tried, but lacked quality practice time and opportunity outside our club meetings. My progress was slow as a result.

And then, one day in 9th grade, a Monday morning, I had the shock of my life. I walked in to school, sat down by Jimmy and them. Jimmy commanded me to cuss, and I did, feeling like one of the boys. He hauled off and hit me. Hard. "Now why did you go and do that for?" I demanded.

"On account of I got saved last night," Jimmy replied. I had been to that church earlier, sat through the altar call there, which was a noisy and stirring event. I guess Jimmy felt he needed to do better. I don't know. All I know is that Jimmy got SAVED, and I mourned that. We had to stop our cussing club. The rules were all changed. Now I too needed to worry more, if possible, about the condition of my immortal soul.

I knew there was supposed to be joy in heaven with all the angels when a sinner repented, but why did it have to be Jimmy anyhow that got saved? Things were moving along just fine far as I was concerned. I doubted if being saved would take with Jimmy, being as by that time I had gotten saved a couple of times my own self without any discernable positive outcomes. But by the time it wore off of Jimmy, I just knew it would be forever too late to resume the care free days of the cussing club.

And it was.

"Mulligan, Party of Three"

Not to make too much of an issue of it, but growing up with a belief that fighting is wrong cramps your social skills development, especially when you are surrounded with vile characters and wickedness of all degrees.

And that is just the way it was, growing up Mennonite in Knoxville. There was lots of wickedness around, but most of the time it just surrounded us, and didn't touch us in a direct fashion. It was sort of funny to watch Cock-eyed Reed and Old Man Eric staggering down the center of the street in their drunken and uncertain ways. We were entertained by the fight across the street when somebody challenged Rudy to come on out and fight rather than being a chicken. "Come on out, Rudy. You-a chicken. You a-scared-a me. Here, hol' my coat." And the deep baritone response: "I ain't-a gonna hol' nobody's coat."

When my brother and me would wander on down Johnson Street, hang a right on Texas Avenue, there were these saloons we would pass by, all careful like, because you could never predict just when someone would get tossed through the door. It was amazing stuff.

Although it never made the newspapers or was reported at home, my brother and I would get mugged on a regular basis as we made our way over to the Boys' Club. The Sear's parking lot was a short cut to the Boys' Club and to losing our lunch money. "Hey boy, gimme-a nick'." A gang of boys on foot could outmaneuver my brother on a bicycle, especially when I was being doubled on it, and boom, there went the lunch money. Again. Somehow the promise that it was more blessed to give than to receive just didn't seem to apply to these situations. And what we wanted to give, we weren't permitted to give. A good fight is what I refer to.

So it wasn't all that much of a shock to move on out into the country west of Knoxville. I already knew how to run away, and tried to stay out of harms' way most of the time. Still it was disconcerting to see people get beat up at school. My heart went out to the guy who got his cap taken from him. "Gimme back my calp," he demanded, but it wound up with him being the monkey in the middle. Then one of the big guys grabbed him around the neck and introduced his head to a car door several times. After that, he decided he didn't want his "calp" very bad anymore. He just sat on the ground and gazed off into the distance, sort of like he was thinking deep thoughts. Oh, that made me mad. If I was able, I would have hurt somebody. But I wasn't and I didn't.

But those daggone old Mulligan boys. They were all cousins and trouble with a capital "T." They banded together and made trouble, knowing that it was one for all and all for one. Derick was in my grade, and wore his hair in a crew cut, which was a sure sign of a tough nut. Tank was big and fat, and caused you to want to go the other direction when he headed your way. Tiny, who wasn't, was not gifted, but pretty strong. Richie, on the other hand, was just pure mean. He had that lean and hungry look, like a copperhead snake, and twice as mean. Explosive and dangerous, a boil ready to pop. No point in being in the same universe with him. He could sense weakness from way far away, and he would go there. Woe unto the target of Richie's meanness.

That is why Derick got away with so much stuff. You tell him something, next thing you knew, there was a meeting of the Mulligans with you in the middle of it. Derick could even wear a short sleeve shirt that looked like a red calico picnic tablecloth. I noticed it but didn't say anything. I may have looked dumb, but I wasn't STUPID. I didn't want to get a flat head over a dumb old shirt that David wore to school one day.

My church friend Ross was fleet of foot, and that was in his favor. If he had enough, he would go and pop Tank a good one and then run away real fast. Tank would get mad, and chase him, but being as he was fat, it would take a while to build up speed, and then, zip, Ross would zag, and Tank would be eating dust again.

That snake, Richie, who will be sorry one day when Jesus comes, one day just heaved a soft ball high in the sky when the school bell rang. We all ran towards the building, but the ball came down right on my head. It hurt. I had pain and anger, because Richie did that just for the heck of it. Something fierce came upon me and strode up to him, and bellowed at him through my tears, "Richie, I ought-a knock off your fool head." And I meant it, too. I'd had it. To this day I think I could have taken him, but never got to find out. He just looked and walked on by, mean, self-contained, and replete with fundamental malice like the low-down, dirty rotten skunk that he was.

To this day, I can't drive down Bob White Road without having to look around carefully, because that is where those Mulligan boys lived. If I never see them again, it will be a day too soon. I will not be responsible for my actions if ever I do see them. I am liable to apply lead-pipe justice to their flea-bitten hides. They darn near ruined me, because I couldn't fight them and get it over with. They were vicious, vile, cantankerous, resolute sinners. No doubt they believed in Jesus Christ, but I never figured they had been properly saved, even once, or even could be, if you really sat down and thought about it. They were just too mean, especially that measly rat Richie.

The other week I returned to Knoxville for a conference. I wanted to show my wife the places I lived growing up as a Mennonite in Knoxville. I called up Ross and Ralph's parents, that telephone number from far back in the archives of memory: WO5-5555. We made contact, and agreed to meet at 5:30 out at Cracker Barrel on Campbell Station Road. Once again, driving those familiar roads, with the furtive glance around - you can't ever be too careful with them Mulligans, eventually turn left to Cracker Barrel. There they were looking not a day older than they did thirty years ago. We had a great suppertime together.

Nature called, and I answered. On the way back to table, I heard the hostess page: "Mulligan, party of three." I don't mean to be overly dramatic here, but when I heard that, boys, I nearly fell out. My anxieties surged as my stomach dropped. How did those Mulligan boys know I was there? What was going to happen now? The fire in my belly has been pretty much dampened and banked in the last forty years, and I really didn't want to have to fight them at this point in my life. All I wanted to do was set down and visit with old friends.

I looked around worried-like, but I never saw anybody that looked like them, except for a fat, runty redneck country boy that looked dumb enough to be a Mulligan, but lacked that essential meanness about him. I ceased looking, and went to my seat, a bit distracted, I know.

I didn't mention this to my wife or to anybody else. Like so many other insults and injuries, I just pondered it in my heart.

Definitive Statements

In some ways, I suppose there is a churlish streak in my way of thinking. There isn't any need to get apologetic about wanting definitive statements to a simple question. Why be content with circumlocution when a straight answer is needed? When I ask a simple question, what I want is a simple answer - boom. That isn't asking too much to my way of thinking, unless you are one of these deep people who feel compelled to seek out hidden layers of complexities in the simplest of questions.

Now, Mr. Smith, our neighbor in Tennessee, could drive you nuts if your quest was to get a quick answer. There was nothing quick about him. He farmed by mule team, Dan and Kate, and plowed his ground with a one-mule walk behind plow, with the reins draped over his shoulder. Dan was the better mule for plowing - he was just naturally more of a one-track mule. You don't operate with racing thoughts when you plow with Dan. You just look at his behind end and say "Gee" or "Haw" occasionally as the need arises, and ponder on the red shale/clay mixture being turned over by the plow.

No, Mr. Smith was not what you could call a speed demon. His every thought, word, and action was measured, preceded by sucking in his hollowed-out cheeks, stroking the unshaven chin, and side-wise glances out of knowing eyes. He was a Kipling-man, one who would keep his head while others were losing theirs. This I saw happen on more than one occasion.

The kind of direct statements I was most comfortable with occurred on Saturday night over at Mr. Smith's house. Being as I grew up Mennonite in Knoxville, we didn't believe in television. In order to see the Saturday night 'rasslin' matches, we would have to scurry over to the Smiths to watch with them. They did not have running water or indoor plumbing, but they did have electricity and a TV. Saturday night with Mr. Smith, his wife Sis, his sister Loretta, and Loretta's son Butch

("I'm blind in one eye and can't see out of the other") was not to be missed. I mean, 'rasslin' was the culmination of the week.

Sis took her 'rasslin' seriously. Lots of unambiguous comments. "Look-a that, ref. Look-a that. Pulling him down by the hair of his head." Cries for revenge were loud and frequent: "Qualify him! You ought-a qualify him!" Suggestions of violence would be offered: "Ought-a tear off his arm and beat him over the head with the bloody pulp." Some of those rasslers were just lawless low-life scum. They would do whatever they could get away with; they would cheat something awful.

When one of the bad ones, like that old Mop Head, would take and run his opponent's eye along the ropes, the agitation in the Smith living room would be just unbearable. That is when Mr. Smith would shuffle around a bit and say, "Boys, if I was able, I would have to get in there and hurt somebody." He was not given to rash statements.

Since Mr. Smith raised hogs and was our neighbor, he would be asked to offer an opinion on the weight of the veal calves or market hogs. None of us had scales, and it was a matter of some consideration for when the animals were the right weight. If you guessed on the light side, you lost money. If you guessed on the heavy side, you lost money as well. It had to be right. I could never quite figure out how to estimate the weight.

We did have one of those weight tapes. You put it around the calf, just behind the front legs, and it would tell you how much it would weigh. But we all knew that was just an estimate.

So we would call in Mr. Smith. "How much you reckon that calf will weigh?" Mr. Smith would look obliquely, stroke, scratch, and spit. He studied the calf real hard. Finally he would pronounce, "You cain't never rightly tell. Sometimes they'll fool you, boys." No matter how much you would press him, he would resort to: "Sometimes they'll fool you, boys."

So the calf would go off to market. Next day, Mr. Smith would amble over to the house. "How much did that calf weigh?" he would ask. When he heard the answer, he would nod wisely and reply, "I 'lowed it would be about that much."

I could never quite figure it out. It seemed that he could have just simply said what he thought ahead of time instead of afterwards. But he had a natural dignity that forbade despairingly motivated comments.

Growing up Mennonite in Knoxville meant that there were certainties. You knew what was right and what was wrong. Some things were just clear. Ambiguities were to be avoided, because a double-minded man is unstable in all his ways. Heresy and apostasy would creep in through the cracks that uncertainties left uncovered. We didn't have money for scales, but that didn't stop us from wanting a certain answer to things, like how much that calf weighs before we took it to market. At least an expert opinion.

Besides, you couldn't blame Mr. Smith if the calf went to market too soon or too late. How do you fight with the comment "I 'lowed it would be about that much." Being a communal people, we sort of wanted to eschew single-handed decisions. There was supposed to be safety in a multitude of counselors. But it was so frustrating to get a definite answer out of Mr. Smith.

Now that I am a sort-of Mennonite and no longer live in Knoxville, there have been ample opportunities to ponder Mr. Smith and his replies. And other replies like his. How well I remember the guy in the auto store who answered my question about if I could get rid of the engine noise in my car radio. He said, "I guarantee you that will probably take care of it." Now what kind of an answer is that? And I MARRIED the mistress of misdirection when it comes to information sharing. "Kathy, is African Vibrations the name of a musical group?" "I got that shirt for you in South Africa."

Like my Grandpa Yoder would moan, "It is enough to make you jump up and down. It is enough to make a grown man weep."

Instead of jumping up and down or weeping, I ought to do like Mr. Smith. There is a time for sucking in your cheeks, glancing around, and in general, slowing down. In reality, many times there just aren't definite statements to be made. And the more definite I have been in my statements, well, generally speaking, the more definitely I was wrong. And, while I am at it, don't some things that are most divisive have the moral equivalence of weighing calves by consensus?

Mr. Smith, my hat is off to you. You are RIGHT. When it comes to guessing weight of animals (and a host of other imponderable questions), the best response, outside of a scales, for example, is to say "Sometimes they will fool you, boys."

Both Sides of the Window

They say that barking dogs don't bite. I don't know about that. I do know for a sure and certain fact that barking dogs can impact your spiritual development. Especially the kind that get started and can't get stopped.

Growing up Mennonite in Knoxville meant that if the church doors were open, you were there. You went early and stayed late. And it wasn't necessarily a burden, because you could run up and down the sidewalk and meet your friends. Wednesday night prayer meetings were without a doubt the best, because while the adults had prayer meeting, the kids got to go the basement for children's meeting with Ruth Byler.

What a treat that was! Ruth was a constant source of comfort, predictability, and stability for us. She had a kind face and she showed a special interest in us children. When we talked to her, she listened with her heart. She loved us. I don't recall her ever saying it out loud to us, but kids KNOW. She was there for us, and that was special. I wonder if it was a burden to her to always be with the kids rather than with the adults. Maybe she preferred it that way.

Children in Knoxville were appreciated. We had Bible School with those wonderful Herald Press Bible School materials. I loved learning about Little Wang Fu of China and couldn't wait until next year until I could make the Jerusalem house like my brother did this year. We got taught the Beatitudes, and other verses, and if we could say them correctly, we got a prize. Man, I worked on that, and squeaked by under the wire one time, even though I hated to say things the way Sister Betsy demanded. Anybody knew the Bible said, "Be ye kind," rather than " 'e 'e kind."

But Sunday nights - man, that was a trial. Nothing for kids except to sit there, and sitting was hard to do. There were these wooden folding chairs that were better than the slat benches. The slat benches would seriously

25

hurt you if you sat on them too long. We weren't long on comfort in those days. You had to be stout of constitution to tolerate Sunday night in Knoxville.

In spite of the seating arrangements, we had pretty good a-capella singing in Knoxville, for being as small of a group as we were. Except we would sing so slowly, and some of the songs, like "Oh, Why Not Tonight" or "Just As I Am" would take forever to sing. Not only did the songs make me nervous, I had the added concern that the Lord would return before we got done with the songs.

Boring is what I remember mostly. It was either be bored to death or be scared to death if you listened. So I tried to elect boredom to keep the anxiety at bay. If you scooted around too much, your mom would pinch your leg and hang on like a broody hen protecting her eggs. Bert would get too restless and his mom didn't pinch him - she would pick him up and haul him outside. We knew what would happen next, and so did Bert, because he would wail out, "Not too hard, mamma."

So to keep from being walloped or pinched, I would entertain myself. Like any good Mennonite church, we had a clock front and center, and that was helpful to time how long I could hold my breath. Who knew when your life might depend on your ability to hold your breath for a long time? Say like as if the Russians were coming to take you away because you believed in God and you could hide and not breathe while they were looking for you. Or if the government wanted to drown you in a vat of water because of your faith, if you could hold your breath a long time maybe they would give up because they thought you were dead already and then you could fool them. It was important to be ready.

Another thing you could do was to lean your head back, gaze up at the tongue-and-groove ceiling boards and relax your eyes. If you did it just right, then the ceiling would get 3-dimensional and it would be like being in another universe. That one took concentration and time, but was preferable to learning about the Great Tribulation and the burning sea of fire that will never go out.

But on hot summer evenings, sometimes none of these tactics worked, and it got so tedious. We didn't have air conditioning, of course. We did have fans from the funeral home and that helped a bit. With the windows opened up, if we were fortunate, a breath of air would come in. But so did the noise. Especially from that little white dog across the street. That dog would bark the entire time, the same monotonous yip, yip, yip, without surcease for the entire church service time. That was a trial.

I know this was an unholy thought, but I wanted to kill that dog. I wanted to at least kick it. Anything to make it stop. It was Chinese torture on University Avenue, that incessant yip, yip, yip, constant as a drop of water on the head of a restrained prisoner. It seemed to be my personal hell, because I don't know that anybody else was affected by it so much as I was. How could they stand it?

Brother Ezra was so glad to see us in church on Sunday evening, bless his heart. I liked Brother Ezra, but it didn't make a lot of sense when he would rhetorically ask, "Where else would you want to be on a Sunday evening than here with God's people?" A number of options came to mind, especially when that daggone dog got to yipping.

And there you have it, don't you? Maybe to have the goodness of being with God's people, you have to contend with the distractions that come from both sides of the window.

Previously published in The Mennonite, *Vol.8, No. 9, May 3, 2005*

Apologies

Growing up Mennonite in Knoxville meant that we couldn't go to any of the school sport events, but we could go to Bible School. Bible School was fun, and we enjoyed it. Even Buddy, who didn't function well in other settings, looked forward to it. "I'm-a gonna go Bi-ba Schoo'," he announced to us at the corner of University and 5th. And it was something to look forward to until I got to 4th grade.

I just knew it would be a bad experience, and I had a couple of years to dread it, because Mabel was always the 4th grade teacher. To get to 5th grade, you had to pass through the valley of the shadow of Mabel. And it was my year.

Don't get me wrong or anything like that. I am sure there were a lot of people who liked her. In her own way, she was likely an honorable person. On second thought, she had to be, because she moved to Knoxville as a Mennonite, and she was married to Clarence, who wore a plain vest with a lot of buttons on it. Clearly she was a person of feeling, but not the kind of feelings that were enticing to a young boy who was dreading 4th grade Bible School.

Probably it isn't fair to blame her for a miserable time in 4th grade Bible School in Knoxville. She was only the teacher. There were these girls there, too, and that by definition spelled trouble. I had already learned that you could get into trouble with adults regarding girls, when it really wasn't any of the adults' business to begin with. I mean, all I did was wiggle my eyes at a cute girl in 4th grade at Lonsdale Elementary School, and said to her, "I dig that car." Mrs. Nelson said in a tone thick with reproof, "Kenny." I felt very conspicuous and flushed with shame in front of that girl and everybody else standing in the lunch line.

So that is why I felt the need to act when four of the girls linked arms and took up the whole sidewalk during recess time in Bible School. I wanted to run down the sidewalk, but there they were, taking up all the space and walking very slowly and talking. Girls were always walking slowly and talking a lot. I tried to be nice, honestly, but it didn't do any good. "Come on," I said to Ralph. Let's get through," and I led the way. We ran right through them, and blew them apart.

Mabel saw it. Mabel called me. I had to go to her while she tried to readjust my attitude. She wasn't very successful, as it wasn't my problem. The problem was with those stupid girls.

"Oh, Kenny, I want you to go apologize," she moaned, with tones filled with grief. Apologize? It wasn't even communion time yet, and furthermore, they shouldn't have been walking like that, taking up the sidewalk. I didn't feel the need to apologize. That was serious activity, and took a lot of starch out of a fellow. And to be so specific about it was beyond the call of Christian duty. The accepted pattern was to be sorry in a global sort of way twice a year, and make a basic boiler plate apology, something like, "If I have done anything to offend someone I am sorry and will you forgive me." This business of doing it Mabel's way was up close and personal, sort of like hand-to-hand combat. No thank you very much. I didn't want to go there. I probably indicated that in some fashion, because Mabel had a reaction.

"Oh, Kenny, this hurts me right here," placing her hand over the center part of her chest. She swayed around a bit, leaned forward in her earnestness, clutching her heart. This did not make a bit of sense to me. I failed to see the connection. Things were getting complicated. I just couldn't see why she should be in pain over something that had nothing to do with her. I wanted to tell her what she could do with her hurt, but I couldn't think of anything.

Besides, I didn't feel the need to apologize, but the ante was getting raise by the second as she began to breathe a bit more quickly and sway around, like a cat with a stomach ache. She normally carried the demeanor of someone who had just discovered a hair in their mashed potatoes, but now she was truly far beyond that stage. So it became a problem for me, even though she was the one in pain. Do I let her die, just so I can be true to myself?

Who was this apology for? For the cause of my own soul? That I seriously doubted, because you apologized when you were real seriously wrong, and being wrong was heavy stuff. We all knew that a bent nail could never be made exactly straight again, and it would never be quite as strong. That is why you didn't want to apologize. It generally was done under some sort of duress, and it was sort of like having winter with no Christmas, this business of apologies. Saying you were wrong, and how sorry you were, and having it hang over you for the rest of your natural life. No sir, it could never be quite the same again.

How I hated the policy of enforced apologies. Just whip me and get it over with. At least once, and probably more, I HAD to tell my brother I was sorry and would he forgive me - and then KISS HIM. That is enough to make you spin around and around, gagging and retching. I can't say that I ever felt much relief after such an episode, just more humiliation and shame.

Before Mabel went into her final death rattle, I decided I better get with the program. So with the same anticipation as someone being introduced to escargot when he knows for a certain fact that it is a snail, I choked out, "I apologize," and sulked away, bent and weakened forever.

Many years later I encountered warmth in the midst of winter. I learned about words of assurance that follow confession. So don't wait around for me to apologize for anything if you are of the firm conviction that now I am a bent nail that can never get straight again.

Wiggle Room

Not that I am obsessive or compulsive or anything like that. I just like to know for sure what we're talking about. If words are used imprecisely, all manner of uncertainties rattle around in my mind. Too much is left up for interpretation.

Take like when we would play 7-Up back in third and fourth grade. Kenny Miller was in my class and then there was me, Kenny Yoder. I loved it when both of us were part of the seven that were up. That way, when someone would look at me and guess, "Kenny?" I could say, "Kenny who? Which Kenny? Do you mean Kenny Miller?" because they had not specified. There was always the chance that they meant the other Kenny. You need to make sure about these things.

In the morning, Mother would call out "Boys." We were just supposed to know what that meant - it was time to get up and get dressed and cleaned up and get ready for breakfast and don't make me have to call you the second time or else. But there was just that edge of uncertainty. Maybe she meant something like, what a surprise. Here are the boys I thought I lost last night. Or sure enough, this is the room where the boys sleep. It was always a possibility that she was just talking to herself. How was I to know for sure, with so many options to choose from? There isn't anything wrong with wanting a bit of clarity about these things.

Growing up Mennonite in Knoxville gave you lots of opportunities to wonder about the actual intent of statements. We sang about the only way to be happy in Jesus was to trust and obey, but that confused me a lot, in that I didn't encounter many people who looked happy in Jesus. And I had no idea what it was to trust and obey Jesus or even if it was a realistic proposition. It felt like an all or nothing proposition, but the more you worked at the all part, the more miserable life became.

Injunctions like be good, behave, and remember who you are left room for interpretation and naturally I interpreted them in ways that left something to be desired. Let's be honest here. You are still behaving even if your behavior is bad. If I was supposed to behave good, that should have been specified. And besides, how much good did you have to do in order to qualify for good behavior? Even saying, "Behave yourself" leaves some wiggle room. Whom else could I even remotely behave? Come on! I could remember who I was, Kenny Yoder - was there any doubt about that - and still come up short in the behavior department. It was just too confusing.

So, when I got to 5th grade, I knew I was in deep trouble because Mr. Sharp was my teacher. He was the only man teacher in the whole school, and we all knew that was worse than getting Mrs.Wertz. And to make it worse, Mr. Sharp was a Catholic, a Roman Catholic. Catholics hated Mennonites and tried to kill them. That was a historical fact. To make it even more frightening, this was in the days when corporal punishment in the school was just a matter of course. I had been initiated to this in third grade, but that was nothing compared to what was in store in Mr. Sharp's class. Men can paddle harder than women.

On the very first day of fifth grade, Mr. Sharp introduced himself to us, and then in a precise style that I learned to respect, he introduced us to The Convincer. The Convincer was a leather shoe sole, probably around size 16. I hadn't learned to cuss yet, so I didn't know what to say that would have been suitable to the occasion. Then he said, "If The Convincer breaks, I have his cousin in the drawer here," and out came a bolo paddle. Boys, I am here to tell you right now, that was just too much for me. I cried. I knew for a sure and certain fact that there would be little wiggle room with Mr. Sharp.

Not only did I cry on the first day of fifth grade, I cried every day for at least 2 weeks. It just wasn't fair. I had just gotten over my fear of Mr. Seeger's electric paddling machine that he had in the office. Mr. Seeger, Colonel Ervin T. Seeger, was the principal, and he had a bald head and shoulders that would hunch up when he

34

would laugh. That was proof enough for me he had an electric paddling machine, and rings on the office walls to tie you up to, just like Roger Benson said. And Roger Benson knew all about things like that. So when The Convincer came sliding out of the desk drawer, I knew it was just a matter of time until we had more than a casual acquaintance. I just didn't know when it would happen. It may be soon, it may be long, but just like the rapture, it was coming, sure as shooting. And like the rapture, I knew I would likely come out on the wrong side of things.

No sir, there was little room for ambiguity when it came to The Convincer. It helped to focus our attention on things that mattered. It helped us to pay close attention when Mr. Sharp explained things to us. Like the day we came up the steps from the lunchroom. Mr. Sharp stopped us and said, "Children, you are walking too loudly. You don't have to make that much noise walking up the steps." He didn't say, "Be quiet." No sir. He showed us. He said, "Watch me," and he walked up and down a flight of stairs. We all watched, still as death itself. I watched his feet, and noticed the frayed cuff of his pants riding across the top of his highly buffed shoes as he precisely feathered his feet on each step. "Now," he said, "you can walk like that." And I am here to tell you right now that we could and we did.

Mr. Sharp paid attention to things that we could and should do. He told me to use my fork at lunch when I was used to eating with a spoon. And I learned to use a fork, real good. And the day we walked to the public library, Mr. Sharp noticed when we passed by a line of black students on the other side of the street. Charlie called out, "Hey, a bunch of chocolate covered gum drops." Charlie had to apologize to our school, our classroom, and to the entire school for black students for his comment. Mr. Sharp could be rather persuasive about these things, and this was 1960 in Knoxville.

I think The Convincer was partly responsible for our willingness to comply with directives, but only partly.

It helped us to focus, and Mr. Sharp taught us the rest. He taught us to observe.

In the fall of the year, he taught us about expansion and contraction. "Now look out at the telephone wires," he commanded one day. "Notice how far down they sag. When it is cold, we will look again and see what happens to them. We will notice how many windowpanes higher they will be. That is contraction." And when it was cold, he put a balloon over the mouth of a milk jug and placed it on the radiator. "We will see what happens when the air heats up in the jar," he announced. But Edwin messed with the jug and it rolled off the radiator and broke into a thousand pieces. Edwin got kindly pale around the gills and we were all paralyzed with sympathy for the hapless Edwin. Mr. Sharp came back into the room and asked, "Who is the culprit?" I paid attention, because that was a new word to me. No ambiguity about that. Mr. Sharp liked to be precise about these things.

He wanted us to have expanded vocabularies. One day we learned about all the different ways police can get you. They can catch you, they can arrest you, and they can chase you. They can put you in jail, they can put you in the paddy wagon. Edwin said, "They can apprehend you." Mr. Sharp smiled and said, "Very good, Edwin." We all basked in Edwin's praise. The sun came out in Mr. Sharp's classroom and glory shone all around. Apprehend was a very advanced word, much more creative than "git." Edwin was destined for great things, this much was clear.

I tried real hard to warrant praise from Mr. Sharp, but I wasn't advanced in vocabulary like Edwin and I wasn't any good in art, although I wanted to be. But one day I drew a picture of a stream of water flowing under a bridge with the reflection of the bridge on the water. I thought the reflection part was creative. Mr. Sharp smiled and placed my picture on the wall. That was as good as it got. He noticed. At that moment, there was no Convincer.

36

It was just Mr. Sharp and me, and I didn't have to cry anymore in fifth grade.

We could explore new words and concepts with Mr. Sharp, and that was fine by him. Like, "The police apprehended the bad guy." One day I came early to school just so I could sit in my seat and watch Mr. Sharp. Then I announced, "I think I have problems." He raised his head and waited. "I am not sure what kind of problems they are. They are not physical, and I don't think they are spiritual." Mr. Sharp waited while I thought about it. I didn't know other words that might describe it. "I don't know, but I think they may be emotional problems." I don't know where that concept came from, nor did I know what it meant. I wondered if Mr. Sharp would help me clarify things a bit. He didn't say anything. He smiled gently, and went on about his business. I sat there in the quietness, and the discomfort that came with me into the classroom seemed to be neutralized by the ambience. I never even once thought about The Convincer.

But it was still there. Oh boy, was it ever. It came out of the bottom drawer on the right hand side of the desk by my own hand, and to my own undoing. And this is how it came to be.

Edwin was an original sort of fellow, a scrawny, self-assured ten-year-old boy with real short hair. He called his mother "Martha," played a trombone, and was advanced for a fifth-grader. We all knew that. But it didn't buy him any indulgence from the purgatory of the paddle. To this day, I don't know what Edwin did, but this I know: Time stood still. Mr. Sharp said, "Edwin, go get it." The birds ceased to sing, the traffic stopped, the wind was still, the wing beats of the angels were silenced. A mighty dread seized our troubled minds. To say that you could hear a pin drop does no justice to that moment in our classroom. I believe if you listened hard enough, you could have heard the music of the spheres, the collision of the molecules of air. Each time Mr. Sharp commanded, "Edwin, go get it," Edwin would just slink his puny frame even deeper in his chair, like there was some exception in the near future if he could just disappear. "Edwin, go get it," and I picked up the hum of the electrons as they buzzed around the nucleus.

I ask you, what is a person to do in such a situation? Edwin wouldn't move, and the situation was getting more perilous by the moment. If somebody didn't do something, and do it quickly, we might all die. How could Edwin just sit there? To me it was crystal clear what was needed. It was The Convincer. Even I understood that. No ambiguity in my mind, at least. It was just unclear about who would go get it, even though Mr. Sharp said, "Edwin, go get it."

My mind was in all a whirl. Maybe Mr. Sharp would be satisfied if he had The Convincer. Maybe that would be good enough, and clearly Edwin wasn't up to doing it. Maybe I could do Edwin and Mr. Sharp both a favor if I just helped out a little bit. So I slunk out of my seat and fetched The Convincer, and took it to Mr. Sharp. He did not thank me. He did not smile. He looked very displeased. This confused me, because, after all, he got what he was asking for. Then he said, "Alright, now you grab your ankles." Holy, holy, holy, Lord God A-mighty. I was in trouble. For once I didn't ponder alternatives. It never even entered my mind to inquire if I could squat down and grab my ankles, or if I could just grab and then let loose real fast. No, there was no metaphorical wiggle room at all. Things were pretty clear to me at that moment in time.

The swish of The Convincer through the air, the sharp CRACK as it landed on my tensed up rear end, the sudden explosion of sharp needles, too numerous to count, racing from my skin to my brain and to all parts of my anatomy. The surprise of the moment helped me to notice the details, adding acuity to the sensations. I went back to my seat, eyes bright with unshed tears, and sat down, avoiding the down cast eyes of my classmates. "Now, Edwin, come HERE," said Mr. Sharp.

Edwin did.

Oh yes, it is good to be precise in one's communications, but I can testify from personal experience that there are times when one should just go with the obvious and not quibble about semantics.

Being There

Sometimes people talk about being at the wrong place at the wrong time. And if you have ever been there, it sure feels like that, like you should have never been close to there at any time. Wrong place, wrong time - final analysis, there you are.

Growing up Mennonite in Knoxville provided lots of opportunities to reflect on "being there." Somehow, to me, it felt like my whole existence was wrong place, wrong time. Especially when those daggone old revival preachers would descend upon us and strike unholy terror into the heart and mind of an imaginative young boy such as I. To this day I stay away from that book of Revelation or Daniel or Ezekiel and eschew eschatology with a devout passion. There are those beasts with many heads, and the whore of Babylon, and the lake that burneth with fire, and any one, all or a combination of them are bound to get you sooner or later. You could try to avoid being at the wrong place at the wrong time, but there wasn't too much chance to avoid it, because there were so MANY wrong places and wrong times. And besides, one could never tell for sure where you stood in these matters.

One thing I knew for sure, there were only two right times to cross over Johnson Street - that was when walking to and from Lonsdale Elementary School. Riding bicycle across Johnson Street or along Johnson Street was by definition out of line. We were not to do this, for no reason that made sense to an 8-year-old boy. And the fact that being on Johnson Street with a bicycle was forbidden made it a treat too good to avoid.

The truth was that playing in the swamp behind the paper mill, and watching Bozo get stranded in the middle of the swamp using a table top as a raft, scouting out the hobo jungle by the railroad tracks, and fishing for crawdads - that was all fun. But Johnson Street worked on the incipient hardness of my heart like a magnet.

41

So there I was, late one summer evening, lolly-gagging up and down Johnson Street when I should have been dodging hobos down in the swamp behind the paper mill, and I heard the chanting sermon emerging from a store front church. If you have never heard good old timey, southern country preaching, I testify here and now, with the certainty born of experience that you haven't been preached at properly. That old style of preaching still attracts me, because of the wonderful extempore skills, the drama, the flair, and the "hah's" that follow every several words when the Spirit strikes, the spontaneous, repetitious "Praise Jesus" or "Bless Jesus" or "Hey-Man" that permeates the sermon like the green liqueur of a crème de menthe parfait. I was sort of sure I was at the wrong place. That was by definition of it being along Johnson Street. But being outside a church, with the door open, while a full scale and full throated revival sermon was going on - I should have known better. I was just there, on the outside and across the street, transfixed by the gyrations and oratory of the preacher.

Then it happened. I was spotted. Wrong place, wrong time. My presence was noted in the sermon, and not just as a footnote, but as the main attraction.

"And look at that boy-hah, a-standing' there-hah, on the STREET-hah. Ain't got no momma-hah. Ain't got no poppa-hah. He's-a tarred-hah. He's-a poor-hah. He's-a cold-hah. An' he's-a HONGRY-hah. What he needs-hah is JEEEEESUS-hah."

Shoot. I was just a Mennonite growing up in Knoxville, that's all, once again being where I shouldn't have been in the first place. I guess one can make thoughts about being habitually at wrong places at the wrong time as symptomatic of moral turpitude. I don't know. But being there makes for some darn good stories.

Divine Elation

Tonight is the 3rd Tuesday of the month. For most people that has no significance, but for me it does. The reason for this is of recent origin. I just happened to be at Flavers, a restaurant in Elizabethtown, on a random third Tuesday of a month and lo and behold, there was a jam session going on, featuring Irish music. It had the feel of being in an actual Irish pub in Clifton or Doolin or some other place on the west side of the island, featuring the authentic version of local music and singing.

So when I found out that this group comes every 3rd Tuesday to sing and play, I decided that would be a good place to be. Good entertainment and a chance to sing along if I happened to know the song or a fragment of it. Faces are getting familiar to me, and I feel free to pound on the table, even though I don't have the rhythmic finesse of the borhan player.

Last month the group of players was small and one of the fellows was in a singing mood. He lifted his voice and sang about being filled with divine elation. In the context of the lyrics, it was clear to me that nothing theological was being referenced. It was an Irish song, after all. But being as the inescapable truth is that I am a Mennonite raised in Knoxville, underneath the reference to the Irish method of socialization, I had to think of things divine.

Being filled with divine elation. I guess we all sort of tried to get there through the path that was straight and narrow, well defined by those who went on before us. We didn't hold too much with showing elation, divine or otherwise. We didn't quake like the Quakers or shake like the Shakers or roll like the Holy Rollers when we prayed through to victory. No, we were to be filled with the joy of the Lord in a less observable fashion. It didn't do to show elation or positive emotion. You could talk about it humbly in measured and solemn tones, always avoiding a prideful or boastful display. It was better to talk about not having divine elation, and being unworthy of it rather

43

than making an assumption that you were there or even on the way.

Occasionally I would get a sense of comfort while singing in church. As a child one of my favorite songs from the Broadman Hymnal was:

> "Jesus, Savior, pi-i-lot me,
> over life's tempestuous sea.
> Unknown waves before me ro-o-oll,
> hiding rock and treacherous sho-o-al.
> Chart and compass ca-ame from Thee,
> Jesus, Savior, pilot me."

I was surrounded by acapella, 4-part harmony, breathing and singing and being in time with my co-religionists, a warm and sacred time.

More frequently the experience was not of singing together but in isolation listening to and interpreting the spoken word. That was cold. And given my natural temperament, I could derive more misery out of a sermon than an egg-sucking dog could get juice from a nest of eggs. It would take quite a few mournful hymns to get me back on track again after being scared to death by a graphic end-times sermon.

That stuff would snuff any vestige or promise of divine elation right out of your body, soul and spirit, chronic and insidious as a minor bleeding ulcer seducing you to think that sub-optimal living was the norm.

A more virulent form of spiritual hemorrhage was the concept of the Unforgivable Sin. We were warned about this, more than once. I didn't know what it was, although I thought it had something to do about grieving the Holy Spirit. But I didn't know how to go about doing that. Unless by simply existing was a form of grievance, and I couldn't do too much about that, now could I? I was just a scared little kid and couldn't figure these things out.

One dark evening, there at 1018 Connecticut Avenue, I sat in the bathtub, and started drawing water for my bath. Being of the frugal frame of mind, I put the stopper in, and turned the hot water tap on. I knew it would take a bit until the warm water would flow. It was possible that some warm water might go down the drain before you got the stopper in. Couldn't let that happen. So, like life itself, one needed to adjust to the cold and hope that warm would come before it got too bad.

Just as the cold water crept up the division of my buttocks, I was seized with a horrific thought. Had I done IT? By IT, I mean the big IT. The Unforgivable Sin. I knew a lot about sinning by age 9, but I also knew that twice a year, just before communion time, you could sort of count on getting forgiven, painful as it was. But what was IT? And how was one to know if IT had been committed, knowingly or unwittingly? That dread had me in a heart lock, and my head couldn't get loose either. Nothing communal in a shallow tub of cold water.

I couldn't take it anymore. No more bath. No more being alone and cold. I had a memory of my mother warming up a blanket by the wood stove, and how we would run into the blanket, and get wrapped up, "all nice and warmy," as we would say. I couldn't ask for a warm blanket because I wasn't cleaned up yet. What I needed was another type of warmth. I wandered around the kitchen a bit, and finally, very nonchalant like, I asked just what the Unforgivable Sin really was. Don't recall much of an answer to the question. I guess I should have flat out asked if I had done IT, but you didn't want to admit to any sort of sin unless there was just no other way out. I just didn't have the guts to be up front and specific about it.

Divine elation - heck - what I had was divine anxiety. This 9-year-old boy managed to subdue the hammer hold on his heart and the abdominal stabs enough so that he could finish up his bath and go to bed, devoting the rest of his life to trying to ignore that unanswered question, figuring there was nothing he could do about it anyhow.

Oh, yes. I tried very hard to get that good feeling I was promised. I got saved a couple of times, got baptized, and even had hands laid upon me in an effort to get the Holy Spirit, but none of those efforts seemed to take, because I neither spoke in tongues nor manifested any evidence of Living on the Higher Plane, or the Spirit-Filled Life. My Utmost for His Highest didn't get me there.

No sir. I have had enough of sitting in THAT cold bath tub by myself. Been there, done that. Don't want any more of THOSE apples. I want that warm blanket.

Maybe I never will get filled with Divine Elation, of either the Irish or the theological variety. That's OK. Once in a while, I will slip in out of the cold, and venture to sing a song. I will sing a song, preferably a-capella, in 4-part harmony. I will wrap myself in the warmth of the community of believers when I can stand it, with a tentative thought that it will be good for me even though I haven't quite cleaned up enough yet.

And I will go to Flavers each 3rd Tuesday evening and eventually I will learn all the words to that song.

"Jesus, Savior, Pilot M," Edward Hopper, pub.1871, Public Domain

Big Trouble with Little P's

My father's schoolteacher was named Irene Zook. Irene Zook must have been a very special teacher, a kind and formative person in the lives of her students. I bet she helped her students mind their p's and q's, but never in my life did I hear a negative comment about Irene Zook from my father or any other students that she taught in her long career at Greenwood (DE) Mennonite School. Just that one comment tells you a lot about the graciousness and influence of this most unusual person. Irene Zook was what it meant to be a teacher, and how students should revere their teachers.

I heard it more than once in the House of Yoder: "If you get in trouble in school, you are in trouble at home." That being interpreted meant if I got a spanking at school, I would get one at home. We were supposed to mind our p's and q's also. With the revered status of Irene Zook the School Teacher figuring significantly in the family story, and what with growing up Mennonite in Knoxville, there was no way I stood a chance against any of my teachers. I didn't have many teachers that even approached the Irene Zook status of pedagogical sainthood. And there simply was no need to speak of the multiple failings of my teachers at home. It just wasn't the thing to do.

My teachers, unlike Irene Zook, were more of the human variety. I guess one could say some of them were quite human. When I got in junior high school, I became acutely acquainted with their failings, and took it quite personally, which is the natural outcome of reading the Martyr's Mirror too much. One had to be on guard, because people in authority, like teachers, could turn on you in an instant, and there was nothing to be done about it. Couldn't even talk about it at home. There wasn't any recourse except to suffer in silence, or if you got the chance, to go underground with your revenge.

When I got in 8th grade, I knew there was trouble ahead of me, because one of the teachers was Mrs. Usher, as rhymes with flusher, which reminds one of a toilet, and that suggests how I thought of her. And speaking of toilets, you had to get special permission to go to the toilet if you were in her class and the call of nature was urgent. She gave the impression that one's bowels shouldn't move and that your bladder should become extra elastic when you were in her class. My classmate Tim not noted for his refinement or high society mannerisms, was less than subtle about his bathroom needs one day. He had to go so terribly bad, and he just begged to go to the bathroom. I bet Irene Zook would have let him go, but no, Mrs. Usher said he wasn't allowed. Didn't matter how bad he was suffering. And it didn't have to do with a little p either. "OK," Tim said very loudly, "I will just sit here and let stinkers." AND HE DID. Oh my goodness, it was just awful. Bouquet de toilette. Quiet but deadly. Even Mrs. Usher noticed. Finally she cleared her throat very dainty-like, and prissed out of the room while saying, "Tee-yem, would yew open a few windies?"

When I say prissed out of the room, that is exactly how she moved. She wore those awful high heel shoes, tight tight tight black skirts, red blouse, red lipstick, and when viewed from behind while walking, she presented like the rear view of a pregnant cow. Her thighs didn't have much freedom of movement. She pranced with prissy diagonal movements from the knees down, counter balanced by alternating thrusts of her hips. I bet Irene Zook didn't walk like that.

And to add insult to injury, Mrs. Usher scolded me one day, with her supercilious expression, customary hauteur, and demeaning demeanor. I thought she was around the corner, and I walked in a very dramatic fashion down the hallway. I think it would do me serious bodily harm to replicate that gait today, but it was enjoyable at the time. Full body involvement was going on. But Mrs. Usher, she of the beady spy eye and general irritability of a copperhead snake, caught me. She descended upon me with that sneer I knew so well. "If ye waunt-a ac' like a mounkey, we'll poot ye in-a caige." Nyah nyah nyah nyah. Mennonites aren't supposed to hate anybody, even enemies and/or torturers, so I wasn't allowed to hate her, exactly. But I was sorely displeased with her.

And how she wanted us to mind our p's and q's. Especially the p's. You had to write the little p just right: _three-quarters a line upstroke_, full loop on the bottom, rounding off the circle of the p, leaving the rounded part at half-staff. That upward flagpole on the little p had to be there. Omitting that was a desecration to sacred precepts of teaching, apple pie and the American Way, and likely was an offense to God as well. She was the angel of death if you didn't make your little p's just right.

My friend Ross was a year ahead of me, and cursive handwriting did not come easily for him. And the necessity for making the little p's a la Usher never quite dawned upon him. Time after time poor Ross had to stay in at recess time and practice making little p's, pages and pages of them. They would start off with the correct hump, but after a couple hundred of them, somehow the flagstaff sunk into the realm of negligence. Oops. There went another recess period. I bet he went a whole school year making little p's during recess. Once in a while, it would get under his skin, and he would write the little p with a great big old huge hump, taking up a line or two.

No sir. There wasn't much to do about this kind of tyranny except to go underground. You could fart in class, write transparent compositions about the misery of certain students in a certain grade in a certain school, or write exaggerated little p's. "I was just making them like you wanted, Mrs. Usher."

My dad has excellent handwriting, thanks in no small measure to Irene Zook, I am sure. I haven't even noticed, or cared, if his little p's were made correctly. If I would have my druthers, I'd rather have happy, Irene

49

Zook kind of memories, rather than being reminded of a toilet every time I write a little p.

The Book

Big books, little books, fat books, and picture books - all my life, books have been important to me. Most of them helped me to escape into a fantasy world where things weren't too bad, and if they were, it was just for a little bit Growing up Mennonite in Knoxville, we had a couple of books that were quite important to us. Of course, first and foremost was the Bible. And the Martyr's Mirror. Then the books read to us, like Pilgrim's Progress, and stories read from Heart Throbs, and the Danny Orlis books I collected.

The one book that I did not have access to, but heard about, was the Lamb's Book of Life. Your name would be written in there by the angels when you got born again, and it was important to get your name there. And also there was a book, maybe the same one, where an account was kept of your misdeeds. The Bible said so. I don't know where it says it, but the preacher could find it. Those two books scared me, as they were sort of mysterious and foreboding. You couldn't check them out or write in a paragraph of explanation. Somebody else did the writing. Didn't seem fair.

When I got to high school, over at Karns High School, there was a book there also. And I got my name in it. My own hand wrote it in. And I don't think it was very fair that I had to write my name in it. It was all because of Mr. Potter.

They had made a rule at our school that chewing gum in class was a bad thing to do. Naturally the best way to promote undesirable behavior is to focus on it, to make a big issue out of it. Take for instance, Mrs. Whaley hated grape flavored chewing gum. This was well known. So what you would do is search high and low for grape flavored chewing gum (do they even make it anymore?) and chew it just enough to have grape flavored breath and then you would dump the chewing gum in her trash can before class, because, remember? You weren't allowed to chew in class. It drove her to distraction, which was altogether total justification to keep on doing it.

They were always making rules at Karns High School, but there were ways to work around them. Like one day, Mr. Potter announced that if anybody brought a transistor radio to school, and got caught, that radio would be taken away and wouldn't be given back anymore, maybe not even at the end of the school year. "Oh, Mr. Potter, " we moaned. "That isn't fair. You can't do that." "Yup, yup, tha's whut it say-es, rot cheer. Take it away. Huhhhhn." "No, Mr. Potter, please don't do that." "Huhhhhhn. Gonna do it," he chortled with twitchy head movements.

There were reasons for that twitchiness. On a regular basis his brief case would get defenestrated, or we would toss one of the mechanical drawing stools down the steps at the end of class, or we would flip off the light switch on the way out of the class. This provided us with a lot of merriment, because he would roar, "Heeeeeyyyyyy!" But he couldn't ever quite isolate the exact offender. There were so many of us. Yes, myself included.

The day the announcement about the transistor radios was made, I felt action should be taken. So I waited until his tortured eyes just passed over Toby and myself, sitting face to face at mechanical drawing tables, with Toby's coat folded up on the peak. I timed it just right. I fiddled with Toby's coat and muttered, sotto voce, "Gotta hide that radio." "Alright, Yoder, bring it here!" "What, Mr. Potter?" "You know what. Bring it here." "I don't have anything, Mr. Potter." "Yoder." "What?" "You better bring it here." "But I don't have anything." "I seen you hide it right there in that coat!" "Mr. Potter, I didn't hide nothing. Believe me." "Did too, and you better bring that radio me right now." "But...."

Mr. Potter stormed to the desk, and fixed me with a baleful gaze that would have been decidedly demoralizing had I been guilty of anything. He was angry, but my conscience was clear, therefore I had the moral advantage. Poor Toby was just sitting there, probably wishing somebody would behave. Mr. Potter lunged for the coat, and I said, "Uh-uh-uh-uh-uh." Mr. Potter shook out the coat like rejected disciples shaking the dust off their sandals. No radio came crashing out. I hadn't broken any rules.

I think he held that against me for a long time. Didn't make sense to me because he was the one who made a fool out of his own self. Had nothing to do with me. Maybe that is why things went a little rough for me at a later time in his class.

All I knew was my name being called out, in tones that did not indicate benediction. "Yoder!" "What?" "You better stop it." This puzzled me, because things were quiet in the room and I was attending to my own business. "Stop what?" "Huhhnnnnn. You know." Huh? Clearly this was going somewhere, but it was a mystery to me. I did not know what to stop, and that makes it hard to do anything different. Three times, with increasing intensity, this interchange took place, culminating with the demand to go to the office and write my name in the book. OK. Didn't know what for, but might as well.

You see, there was this book down in the principal's office, Dr. McAllister's office, where you had to write your name if you committed an infraction. Nowadays, that doesn't seem to be such a big deal, but back then, as a Mennonite growing up in Knoxville, one didn't know for sure what this could lead to. But it would likely lead to something, and that "leading to" process was best avoided. Besides, Dr. McAllister was a most eccentric duck. He had been in Inn-d'ya, and he like talk about it. "Inn-d'ya. Ah-hh-hhh. Inn-d'ya." I didn't know what he was capable of, other than going orgasmic over India, and paddling recalcitrant students. That book at his office made me nervous.

You have to appreciate this situation from my perspective. If I was going to have to write my name in the book for doing something I did wrong but didn't know what it was, well, I was clearly in deep trouble. I knew once this pattern of writing my name in a book got started, it could very easily become a repetitious process. But at least I should know what I had done wrong. But you could never know. Maybe it was like that Lamb's Book of Life, and I suspected my page was pretty well filled up by that time, with small writing and writing sideways on the margins all scrunched in. Maybe the angels would have to put in a few extra pages for me. And like with Dr. McAllister's book, I doubted the angels had erasers, either.

On the way down to the office, I needed to settle my nerves, so I stopped by the white porcelain water fountain, with the spring loaded spoked faucet turner on the side. As I went to swallow the water, it hit me. I HAD CHEWING GUM IN MY MOUTH. Dang! That was what this was all about. I opened the note Mr. Potter wrote to the principal. Sure enough, in Mr. Potter's characteristic scrawl was written the indictment: "Chewing gum. Potter." I thought I would stroke out on the spot. Monumentally unfair. I had been snookered, without a chance to correct my behavior, assuming I would have wanted to. But at least I felt I deserved a choice in the matter.

I fumed down the hallway to the principal's office, thinking I could just sneak in, write "Kenny Yoder" and sneak out again. This was not to be. I met Dr. McAllister, he of the suit, and drawly, nasal appreciation of India. "And what are you here for," he said, as if he really cared about how unjustly I had been treated. "Dr. McAllister, that Mr. Potter...." I sputtered, choking on my fury. "That Mr. Potter..."

I had an epiphany. Protestation of any sort was not going to be helpful to me in the long run, or in the short run, for that matter. Dr. McAllister's eyes narrowed, and he said, "Ah..." "Oh, OK then, I will just write my name in that book." "Very good choice, Kenny," said Dr. McAllister.

I am sad to say that writing my name in Dr. McAllister's book did not help me become a better citizen, a more humane person, a better self-disciplined student.

54

No. My name was in the book, with no notation about extenuating circumstances. It occurred to me that since my name was in the book, I might as well be worthy of that distinction. I got sneaky in Mr. Potter's class.

The best part is, he noticed! "Yoder," he roared at me one day. He mostly roared at me. "Yoder! Other people are open with their meanness. You, you are sneaky about your meanness."

YES!

Life On the Back Porch

Even though I grew up Mennonite in Knoxville, and we were by definition supposed to be a different people, and not to do things like the world did, we still had a front porch AND a back porch when we lived at 1018 Connecticut Avenue.

Front porches enhanced social amenities. We, our neighbors included, were not quite in the social class that allowed for sipping mint juleps while lazing on the white wicker furniture on the front porch. No, that wasn't us. We did have a glider on the front porch, and sometimes we actually visited there. One of our neighbors up the street would sit all day long on his front porch, watching us roller skate up and down Connecticut Avenue. That was a feat of some agility and daring, as the sidewalk was crumbled in certain spots, tree roots elevated slabs of concrete, and there were sudden changes in the surface. To come zipping down the sidewalk invited disaster, which happened on occasion. That front porch neighbor would sit there and laugh and laugh like it was funny. "Har har har. OH har har har." I failed to see the humor in little kids bouncing down and nearly breaking a hip. I guess one could say that in our neighborhood, we were short on gentility and civility.

Now, while front porches, in the mythology of southern living, had a connotation of conviviality, back porches were something else. Back porches were out of the public eye, and life was much more authentic there. That is where you put the deep freeze, wash machine and pots of dried up geraniums. Our pack porch was walled off on one side by kudzu vines. That vine grows up to 18 inches per day and drowns out groves of trees and tears down telephone lines, and it sure made a substantial visual barrier from the alley side of the house. This was both a good and a bad thing.

It was a good thing because you could hide out there and peek out and see what those old boys across the alley were doing. Those boys were barely civilized and I tried to help them out, mostly through recreational fighting, to become morally responsible individuals. I admit to being a bit conflicted about this, because on the surface, this activity didn't seem to fit strictly within the Mennonite understandings of faith and practice, but the need to correct the behaviors of those old boys across the alley took precedence. And since there were more of them than of me and my brother, we needed the concealment of that kudzu vine to survey the relative safety of venturing out into the back yard. Most of the time it was safe. The closer you got to the alley, the more vulnerable you were to attack. Well, actually, the more available they were for assault. That figured in as well.

In our battles, we tried to hold to the high ground, which meant we would shinny up to the roof of our shanty and heave bricks over into their shed. But they fought dirty by throwing rocks back at us, with disquieting accuracy. I wish they hadn't of done that, because that seriously compromised the instructive quality of what we were trying to do.

Now my brother, he was not given to rash action. He was cool under fire, and thought creatively. One day, he beat a strategic retreat, and reappeared with the lid off of Mother's Maytag washer-wringer. It had a knob in the middle, and made an excellent shield. This represented advancement in defensive weaponry, even though I am just about sure Mother would have disapproved on the basis of frugality and theology. I thought I deserved to use it myself, but he said I should go and find my own shield. But we only had the one wash machine. Wasn't fair. That particular idea was short lived, as you had to peek around the edge to throw your rock. It just so happened that one of those old boys across the alley threw a rock just as my brother peeked out and it scored a superficial furrow alongside his head. He produced the sounds of mortal agony, and headed towards the back porch to regain his composure. Afterwards we agreed that those old boys across the alley didn't fight fair, because they hit him, and right in the head, and probably it was a sharp piece of glass that could of taken out his eye.

Back porch living got real at times, with no obvious signs of grace and mercy. Not that I would have recognized them at that time, even if either one of them had snuck out from under the porch and bitten me right square on the rear end. Life back there was raw and unpretentious. Like one day I was denied entry into the house and had to strip down to my underwear and beyond and put on new clothes. All I did was kick a can down the street on the way home from school, and unlike your regular beer cans, this had a thud as you kicked it, and it skittered in an unpredictable fashion. I guess I should have noticed that the end of it was punched open and that it was getting lighter as time went on. I noticed a smell, but didn't pay no attention to it. When I got home and tried to get in the back door, my mother snapped to attention. I guess a teensy bit of the beer splashed on my clothes. I was banished out of the house for good unless I changed my clothes. Now you talk about embarrassing. Brad and them next door were probably watching. I was a forlorn and miserable wreck, caught in the throes of indecision. I seriously considered spending the rest of my natural life in my stinking clothes on the back porch, but I was wise enough to know this would not be well received. So I had my first episode of public indecency, right there on our own back porch, all at the command of my mother.

That back porch clearly had its disadvantages, like being turned into an impromptu (un)dressing room. Also, it was a clear shot from Bradley's back porch to ours. Which was a life-threatening situation, because one winter day I was standing on the back porch with my bib overhalls on, and Bradley up and hurled a snowball at me. When I say snowball, I mean that in a relaxed sense of the word. It was made out of what was once snow, but with the cold temperature combined with a wet snow, by the time he got done packing it into a fist sized missile, it was an ice ball. In my naïveté, it never occurred to me that doom was headed my way. But it was, with great velocity. It hit me just above the bib, splattered like a dum-dum bullet, and a great quantity of the ice ran down inside of my bib overhalls. I shed a lot of tears and created a high-octane racket. But since Bradley was older and bigger than me, I just had to bear it. It was not a happy day.

Our neighbor on the other side, Roger Benson, also had a back porch of misfortune. He was given to telling lies and generalized disobedience. When we would hear Mrs. Benson shout, "Roger Benson, you git here, right now. I'm-a gonna whup you, right now," we would run in the direction of his back porch. Mrs. Benson would be hiding behind the door of the back porch to get in a few good licks before Roger Benson managed to make it entirely into the house. He had to run the one-woman gauntlet. But he was brave and could take it, because he used to be a full-blooded Indian, and in order to turn into a white man, he had to stay in the house seven years without ever going outside. This was indubitably true. Roger Benson said so. He knew how to endure torture without making a sound. Besides, as Roger Benson confided to us one day, "Momma don't hurt."

Roger Benson's back porch episodes were somewhat predictable, even to him. One day he knew that he was going to get it, even before Mrs. Benson started shouting. He took the swat part of a fly swatter and placed it in the back of his jeans, just for insurance. Sure enough, a few minutes later, we all heard, "Roger Benson, you git here..." We followed the internal sounds of the house from the outside, traced them to Roger Benson's bedroom, and crouched below the window to listen.

What we heard was not silence. Neither was it indications of stoicism. No, what we heard was rapid-fire swats, and Roger Benson saying, "OO-OO-oo-oo-lu-lu-lu-lu." We were shocked, but secretly amused.

After a while, Roger Benson came sauntering out of the house, all casual, but to the keen observer, he also seemed to be just a bit subdued.

"Hey Roger, I thought you said momma don't hurt," one of us commented.

"Shut up," said Roger Benson.

Adjust Accordingly

I know this was small minded of me, and I have repented, but the fact of the matter is that I got embarrassed by my mother when I was growing up Mennonite in Knoxville. Actually, this was a double dose of embarrassment, because, first of all, just being Mennonite in Knoxville was embarrassing enough being as I would have to sit on the sidelines when the rest of the kids at school learned to dance in gym class. We didn't believe in dancing. We didn't believe in a lot of things that set us apart from the rest of the crowd, fun things like cussing, recreational fighting, and having television.

And the things we did believe in had certain drawbacks. We believed in being different and being depressed. Both of these things were signs of true spirituality, faithfulness, and maturity, because it showed you were not being frivolous about faith. One needed to take matters of faith very seriously.

So I adjusted to being embarrassed all of the time, whether it was called for or not.

Bread was a source of embarrassment for me, and this snuck up on me quite unaware. You see, my mother would bake bread, and it was absolutely the best bread in the world. The dough would get all nice and puffy, and the taste was simply beyond description. I could hardly wait for the bread to get out of the oven so I could cut off a big huge slab of bread and let the butter melt into the slice.

My first inkling of trouble was when mother came home with a 25-pound bag of flour, and not in the kind of bag that you would get in the grocery store. This was a brown bag, sewn shut at the top like a bag of cow feed. It was commodity flour that mother got her hands on somehow.

Commodity foods, like flour, dry milk, dry eggs, and cheese. I suspect Mother wrangled some sort of trade with some people living in The Projects. The dry eggs tasted awful, and so did the dry milk, but we adjusted to it. There wasn't an option in that matter.

But the bread made with commodity flour tasted wonderful. I was curious about how bread was made, but the instructions were rather vague at best: Make dough with some flour, bubbly yeast, a bit of shortening, a little liquid. Knead the dough until it is right. Let the dough rise until it is done. Punch it down several times. Put your hand in the oven to see if it is hot enough. Bake until the top of the bread makes a certain sound when thumped. If I offered to help, I got told I could help best by staying out of the way. Now this was not embarrassing to me, it was simply a statement of fact.

The embarrassing part came later. One day I discovered that Mother was putting extra ingredients in the mix. Things like left over mashed potatoes, left over oatmeal from breakfast, left over squash. This was outside the rules of bread making, as I understood it. Plus, if I knew some of the extra things included in the dough, what about things I didn't know? Left over cat food? It provided impetus to clean up my plate at mealtime, because the left over scraps could wind up in the next batch of bread.

Oh, it was awful, not knowing what you might be eating. But the bread tasted so good. I just couldn't dwell on it too much. I needed to disconnect my imagination from my taste buds, sort of the way that natives that ate ants and grub worms surely had to do.

And when visitors came to eat supper with us, I lived in fear that someone would ask what made the bread taste so good. I would just die if my Mother would answer, all casual like - "Oh, I just threw in a bit of succotash and left over oatmeal that was starting to get moldy." It never happened, BUT IT COULD HAVE.

When I grew up and got to be thirteen or so, I could see things a bit better. I ceased to be embarrassed by unusual bread ingredients. I stopped thinking about what might be slipped in - things quite outside any known bread recipe.

I got curious how this bread baking process went. "Mother," I asked, "how do you go about making bread with left over vegetables?" "Oh," Mother replied, "you just adjust accordingly." Adjust accordingly. What got adjusted? And how much? I never figured it out. I took it you were supposed to adjust something until it was right. I knew what tasted right, but didn't have the slightest concept of how or what to adjust accordingly to GET it right.

Adjust accordingly. I had to adjust to being an outsider at school and in the neighborhood, but I never quite got it right. It didn't feel right; it left a bad taste. There was a principle involved here - you weren't supposed to adjust too much, because that was compromise, and compromise led to apostasy. But that rule didn't apply to making bread. It made the bread good every time, but it wasn't supposed to be a way of living. It was so confusing.

I tried to make recipe bread when I was out on my own, but it never "got right." I couldn't adjust accordingly to make normal bread, let alone the more creative varieties using left over mashed potatoes.

Adjust accordingly. I suppose it is a good thing if you can do it.

Fractions

In spite of all good intentions, I had trouble keeping up with the Least Common Denominator and the Greatest Common Multiple when I was in Ball Camp Elementary School. Adding and subtracting fractions was just hard work and didn't seem to make a whole lot of practical sense to me. I could understand the concept of a sixth of a pie, because my mother would cut a pie into six pieces, just as even as could be. It make sense that in a family of six, that is the way you would cut a pie, and one piece plus another piece make two pieces. Two sixths. That was simple enough. Trouble was, that was the incomplete answer. Teacher said so. The complete answer was one-third, because two goes into two once and into six three times and that is why. I tried to see it from the teacher's point of view. Teacher said if you have two sixths side by side, they equal one third, one third of a pie.

I don't know what family she grew up in. Certainly not mine, as there wasn't too much time to contemplate pieces of pie. You ate it, and you were concerned that your piece of pie wasn't any smaller than your brother's. One did not consider comparing two pieces of pie side by side directly. You would never get two pieces of pie, even if you were real hungry for it.

On a theoretical basis, I grudgingly accepted the fact that two pieces of pie made a third, but only under certain circumstances. It could be three eights. So what happens if you add one third and three eights of a pie together, and which is a bigger piece? We needed to know these things, and to figure these things out, we had to work with the Least Common Denominator and the Greatest Common Multiple and Reducing Fractions.

Oh, that was hard work, because in my efforts of finding things in common between a seventh and a ninth just taxed my brain to the to the point of insolvency. I couldn't for the life of me understand why they had sevenths and ninths to begin with. I guess it was to make me a better person, but I saw lots of people getting through life without ever in my hearing exclaim over the marvels of adding three sevenths to four ninths and then taking away half of it, and how much would you have then. It was just too disconnected, all those little slivers getting littler all the time until you didn't have much pie left over at all. All that work and so little pie.

And the more you learned, the worse it got. Generally, when you multiply things, like horses and feet, you get more feet. Six horses and four legs per horse. Six times four is twenty-four. Not so with fractions. You get less, because one half times one fourth is one eighth. And dividing fractions gives you more pies. That doesn't make any sense whatsoever. And before you can divide fractions, you need to invert and multiply, but before that you needed to make complex fractions first. So many steps, so many places to get it wrong. Sometimes you cross-multiplied and other times you didn't. And after you were all done, reduce and don't leave it complex.

I was more or less prepared for the futility of fractions, having grown up Mennonite in Knoxville. We knew we were part of something bigger than ourselves. It was just the adding to and dividing from that challenged us to distraction. How do you add six Yoders and three Stoltzfuses to scads of DeLoziers, Prestons, Ames, Laidlaws, and Carpenters, along with an occasional Wright? The adding and dividing seemed to be a constant variable, and a pie paradigm didn't seem to fit real well when applied to church life in Knox County.

There seemed to be an awful lot of anxious energy about these irregular pieces of pies, made in the foreign pie plates of Knox County, compared to pie plates from the Shenandoah Valley. They just didn't match up very well at all. Then there were the Scottdale pie plates, and worst of all, the Western Mennonite ones. Just awful how many sizes and shapes there were all over the place, and none of them didn't seem to want to fit together very well. Not fitting in, church-wise, was a bad thing. But then sometimes, fitting in, church-wise was a bad thing, as well. I should have known that dealing with school fractions would be hard.

And it was. It was tedious and non-fulfilling to wrestle with fractions of all sizes and denominations and trying to make them get to the correct answer. I used to get some wildly improbable answers, but you could never tell for sure, when adding complex and irregular fractions. There were so many uncertainties along the way that I just got messed up.

Eventually I came to peace with fractions in sixth grade. I discovered that you need to make complex fractions first from simple fractions, and then turn one of them upside down and multiply if you want to divide. I figured out how it worked. I stood there by the window in Mrs. Ranger's room, and held my paper on the window glass and did several problems in a row. Glory, glory, hallelujah. It worked. I found the light. I found the way. That is the truth. And I became suspicious of leftover fractions that didn't look right, somehow. They needed to be reduced, or something terminal happened to them along the way.

In short, I commenced to worry less about fractions, and got sort of comfortable with both the idea and the reality of D's in arithmetic. Subsequently, Mrs. Usher ruined my high school education by decreeing that I was general material instead of college prep material. This meant that I went to classes in the basement of the high school with kids that were in school because the law said they had to be, and the sooner they would drop out, the happier everyone was. I guess that is where she figured I deserved to be. Stupid fractions.

But in spite of them fractions, I can count my money, do my taxes, fight over hospital bills, and record what part of the bill is deductible or co-pay or no-pay or all-pay. And I eat as much pie as I want without worrying about the ratio of the part to the whole. Yoo-hoo, Mrs. Usher, you of tight skirt, vicious disposition, and disapproving mouth pursed in an "O", like the anal orifice of a tomcat, here I am. And I don't give a hoot about you and your fractions.

And this proves it. Couple of years ago I attended a memorial service over west of the Susquehanna River, in Mennonite country. I try to either stay out of there, or if perforce I am there, I work real hard to be a common denominational factor. I don't know my way around that territory, and you never know when you will step on a theological landmine, a Venus Fly Trap looking for fresh meat. Alas, it was not to be. One fellow, with a vigor that belied his age, shivered with excitement as he talked with me. "Now what is your name?" he asked. Oh boy. In Mennonite Land, my name betrays me every time. "My name is Yoder." "Oh, Yoder. You must be from Bellwill." "Nah, huh-uh, my people, they come from Ohio, Northern Ohio, you know, Holmes County." "Well, there's lots of them. And lots of fractions, too," he said with sadness. "Fractions here and there. Seems like everybody is in a fraction, somehow. There are just too many fractions."

We pondered fractions for a while, and I dreaded the next question which was sure to come. "Now, which fraction are you a part of?" he asked, in a way that demanded a clear answer.

I took a deep breath, and said, "Why, the right one, of course." We both laughed and parted as friends. But I still don't like fractions.

Or factions, for that matter.

Double Talk

They said the angels kept track of all the words you spoke, and you would have to give an account for any idle words on the Judgment Day. That is why you weren't supposed to cuss. Those were idle words; they weren't needful, according to the celestial editors that oversaw these things. No amplification, no beautification of verbal communication, no nothing except for the basic facts. This mandate was boring and frankly at variance with the cultural norms of Knox County, Tennessee.

Clearly, ever who invented Mennonites did not grow up in Knoxville, because there, if one word was good, two was better. Names, for example. We all knew it wasn't Joe. It was Joe Billy, and his wife was Laura Sue. If a name has a trailer attached to it, the sound just rolls off the tongue better. It sounds better, and gives an internal sense of completion than one word flapping around there all lonesome-like. It is an issue of rhythm and intonation, with each segment adding to the pleasure of the whole. It gives a sense of being at home. Nothing idle about those words.

I expect the angels were more concerned about the words that made preachers and parents get twitchy. Words like ding, dang, darn, dern – stuff in that category. This put me in a real bind because, in East Tennessee, words were so entertaining when put in combination with each other in creative and insightful manners. That is why I thought it was much more entertaining to roar out, "Open the blink-eyed, bag-stabbing door" rather than simply say "Open the door." My parents did not approve, and I am sure the angels wept as they recorded those words. In the dark of the night, I had time to wonder how I would give an account, knowing that the angels likely did not have much of a sense of humor.

The fact of the matter was that a no was not designed to stand alone, neither a yes, unless you were from Yankee land. A no was better expressed as, "Naw, huh-uh." Better yet was, "No-sir-ee Bob." The first word set the theme, and the following words were like conversational oil, to help the main point get across. They provided punch, reinforcement, and clarification. It wasn't polite to be too abrupt with things.

Not that I ever got the chance, being as I grew up Mennonite in Knoxville, but if a fellow wanted to say tender words to his girlfriend, he wouldn't just say baby or honey. No sir. It was better to say things with redundancy, like sugar pie or honey bunch. How could that be offensive to the angels? The more you can string together, the more impressed the girl would be, as any daggone stupid old fool would know. That is why I practiced for years in private until it could roll off my tongue real smooth-like: "Kathy-honey-sugar-sweetheart-darling." That is guaranteed to leave your woman overwhelmed with your love and breathless with desire.

Repetition is the key. If a good thought comes out, it is worth being heard a second time. The preacher said, "The life is in the blood. Did you hear what I said? I said, the life is in the blood." That makes the point, although I must admit I am not quite sure what the point was. But I remembered it. That proves that anything worth saying is worth saying again.

Single, abbreviated sounds are just foreign to the ear and tongue of anybody raised in the parlor of gentility and civility. Several weeks ago I attended Mennonite Health Assembly in South Carolina, and they served cheese grits. Most Mennonites wouldn't know how to identify a grit if it ran around buck naked through your neighborhood truck stop, much less know how to pronounce it. It is not "grits." Any word that had "-it" in it has developed an extra syllable, roughly like "ee-uh." You can't write it exactly, but instead of "grits" you need to say something like "gree-uhts." Not because it is weird or back woodsy or anything like that. It is just the way it is. Anything else is counterfeit, and lacks capacity for tonal polishing in the delivery. Go ahead and practice it on a number of "-it" words. You will see what I mean. It just works better. Authenticity is the way to go, here.

Preachers knew about this, and used this technique all the time, and I doubt the angels got bothered about it. They would say, "The Bible says..." only it sounded more like, "The Bi-i-ble say-es..." You got to get it right. Yes sir, doubles make it better. There is a glottal stop there: Bi-i-ble. And the tonal changes: The Bi (regular) i (higher) ble (regular) say (regular) es (lower, and slowly slide up to regular).

Doubles just make things clearer. You would never say little. It had to be wee tiny. Better yet was to say wee tiny little old thang. Same thing with big. Big. That doesn't say nothing. It doesn't communicate. Great big huge dog gives you a picture of what you are dealing with compared with a wee tiny little old thang. You could kick a wee tiny dog and get away with it, but a great big old huge old dog would tear your leg off right up to the knee if you was to try it.

Teachers were always pesting us about double negatives, and how bad it was to use double negatives in a sentence. It was improper to say, "I don't got no pencils." You were supposed to say, "I don't got any pencils." Dang. Only someone who thought Boston was the center of the universe would come out with something like that. "I haven't any pencils." You would rather die a thousand deaths than try to get by with that kind of so-called proper talk. There isn't a thing wrong with double negatives, and all this stupidity about a double negative making a positive is just double talk, because two wrongs don't make a right. So how could two negatives make a positive? The more negatives you pile together, the more stronger the complaint. "I di'n't. I di'n't say nothing. I di'n't NEVER say nothing, neither."

I tell you what. If you want to be parsimonious with your words, go ahead, shrivel up and die on the conversational vine. I will thrive with redundancy and embellishment, and luxuriate in the sound and cadence of good old down home talk. My soul yeans to hear it again, like a dry and parched ground longs for rain. I just can't get enough of it.

73

Angels, go ahead. Get your pens ready, because I will recite a line from a favorite hymn, "How Firm a Foundation." It had to be written by somebody born and bred in the South.

The soul that on Jesus still leans for repose,
I will not, I will not desert to its foes.
That soul, though all hell should endeavor to shake,
I'll never, no never, no never forsake!

If you get scrupulous, and try to work out what that last line really means, and match up the negatives and switch them around – well you have just done gone and wasted your time, as anybody raised in Knoxville will tell you that line means you are in pretty good hands.

"How Firm a Foundation," pub. 1783 Public Domain

Suffering in Style

We called him C.J., because he had deep feelings about his given name. And if I had his name, I am sure I would have had objections also. Being called "Kenny" was bad enough, but to be named "Courtney Jayne" was insult beyond belief.

C.J. and his family showed up at church once in a while. They hadn't grown up Mennonite in Knoxville, but were trying to get connected at church. I never quite understood why they of their own free will would want to do that. If you get right down to it, being Mennonite in Knoxville would certainly have been a challenge for them.

We used to run around with the Strong boys, C.J. and Kurt, and it was always an adventure. They were tough kids and nobody dared mess with them. Kurt carried a knife, and would pull it if he felt like it. He was quick about it. This I saw happen and was quite impressed. There was this great big mean old junk yard dog that came snarling and growling at us one day, with its short hairs standing on end. I was scared to death, but Kurt, he whipped out his knife, quick as lightening, and snarled his own self: "Come on here, dawg. I'll cut-ye th'oat." You know what? That dog backed down.

I wondered if having a name of C.J. Strong, and having a short-fused, knife-packing brother created moments of indignity for C.J. I am sure there were moments of discomfiture for that poor old boy, untouched by positive by-products of suffering.

I knew it was godly to suffer, especially if you could do it for your faith, but personally, I could not find much virtue or pleasure in it. The Bible said you were supposed to count it all joy if you could suffer for Jesus' sake, and the Martyr's Mirror had these incredible pictures of people suffering terrible things with very joyful expressions. I couldn't make the connection.

I didn't want to suffer at the hand of Kurt and his knife by standing up for Jesus, like a soldier of the cross, especially when Kurt and C.J. did things that we weren't allowed to do, like cuss and pick up cigarette butts off the side of the road. It just didn't seem to be a wise thing to do, but I felt like I wasn't being true because I didn't get cut. But I did cause Kurt to get a major slice one day, and I didn't even mean to.

We were visiting over at the Strong's, and me and my brother, C.J. and Kurt went exploring in a metal culvert running under the road. I was deep in the belly of the thing, and Kurt had gone on out and was standing at the end, examining a jagged edge. It must have been a wasper or a mud dauber come flying by and it scared me real bad, and without wanting to, I jumped. This was not a wise move, because there were these bolts hanging down from the culvert, holding sections together, and as I jumped, I impaled one of them right into my scalp.

I did not rejoice in this at all. I did not have time to compose myself and render a blissful expression. I brought shame upon myself and the whole Anabaptist movement by screaming out loud, a horrific wail, amplified in the bowels of a metal culvert. The sound bounced around inside, nearly deafening those of us inside the pipe, then it shot out both ends like an aural cannon, bringing destruction in its wake. Kurt was there, unaware of what was about to come his way. When that subterranean howl issued from the throat of the tube, he, being caught unawares, leapt skyward. For him this was not good, because that jagged piece of metal on the lip of the culvert caught his finger. It made a deep cut in his skin.

It made him mad. I figured that out by what he said.

I wished I could have suffered more stylistically, but I hadn't learned how to do that yet. My education in suffering was just beginning. It took Mrs. Baker to show me, by precept and example, that there is more to suffering than silence, or screaming, for that matter. Suffering in silence does not have many benefits. What is the use of suffering if you can't get some attention, some mileage out of it? There is no future in weeping alone.

You need to have an audience, witnesses to your life situation. Man was born to sorrow, and one needs to become a visible member of the fellowship of suffering. No, suffering is an art form that needs to be developed over time, and Mrs. Baker was the grand dame of mortal misery.

Paul and Silas did not have anything over her. They rejoiced in suffering just at midnight in the Philippian jail. Mrs. Baker could do it morning, noon, and night, without surcease. Oh, how she suffered, and she did it so well that you just had to admire her style and technique. I got to hear about it on a regular basis, since we would pick her up and take her to church with us on a Sunday morning.

"Law," she would start. "I have suffered so bad with this laig. Kenny, come on over here and he'p me lift my leg up in the car. Not too fast, now. There ye go. Thank-ee. Oh, how I suffered. I went to the doctor, and the doctor said, 'I don't see how you stand the pain. The average person couldn't take the suffering like you do. I don't see how you do it. That is the worst case I ever saw.' They ain't nobody suffered like what I'm suffering." I listened intently, because this was not the way Mennonites in Knoxville suffered. I was being offered new vistas into the way of dealing with pain.

I suppose there are societal benefits in bearing one's burdens in silence rather than overloading the environment with emotional incontinence. They say it is a mark of maturity to be stoic when one is beset with adversity. There might even be a theological justification for quiet acceptance of suffering as a mark of the Spirit Filled Life, and being mournful about it in a joyful kind of way.

No, I am not a fan of suffering, especially when it affects me personally. This is a fact. Actually, I am temperamentally quite unsuited to be listed in the Martyrs' Mirror. That session in C.J. Strong's culvert convinced me of that, once and for all. But I will applaud those who can do it with flamboyance and style.

77

Say What?

I am not saying they are any better or any worse, but Mennonites in Lancaster County, The County, Pennsylvania are *different*. Growing up in the small pond of Mennonitedom in Knoxville, I just assumed that all Mennonites of the proper variety were sort of alike. And Mennonites in The County sort of prided themselves in being proper. That is why it was such a shock to me when I went to a boarding school in The County for the last two years of high school. I thought I would fit in better than I did back at Karns High School, that I wouldn't be as likely to be led astray by undesirable influences, safe in the bosom of righteousness. I had great expectations.

What a naive thought. I should have known better. Kipling said that east is east, and west is west, and never the twain shall meet. I say Mennonites from the South can meet Mennonites from The County, but not without turbulence.

Mennonites in The County acted like there wasn't anything worth noticing outside of Lancaster. Those daggone myopic toads didn't know there was a difference between Tennessee and Kentucky. They just knew I was foreign, and reminded me of it frequently. "Oh, that's right. You are from KEEEEEN-tuck-eeeee. Ah-ha-ha-ha. Isn't that where HEEEEEEEL-billies are? Ah-ha-ha-ha snicker snicker." They couldn't even say Tennessee right. It is TENNessee, not TennesSEE. Made me want be an automatic parrot and shout in their ear without surcease: "Lan-CAS-ter, Lan-CAS-ter, Lan-CAS-ter." They got twitchy unless you said it right: LANK-us-tur.

There are different standards of conduct up there, different ways of being right. If you are really interested, it takes generations to master the code of rightness. The main difference is that Mennonites in The County were infested with a virulent and contagious brand of pernicious religiosity, rife with rules, replete with regulations and devoid of grace. They took their religion real serious, even more so than we did in Tennessee.

Moreover, there was competition for being either the most holy or most indifferent, and Lancaster Conference had The Discipline to lay things out. And then that school had its own set of rules to make sure nothing slipped between the cracks. It didn't make no sense to me then, and it don't make no sense to me now why it was so important that the band on the prayer veiling needed to be 1-1/4" wide, and would be measured to make sure it was not 1-1/8" wide. This is the truth. What did The Discipline have to do with "...holiness, the road/which we must take/to dwell with God"? I guess a lot, because there had to be a principle involved there somewhere.

For a Mennonite growing up in Knoxville, it was easy to know about the most important thing, getting saved. You just got saved and that was it. Jesus gently called the prodigal home. You got saved and got the Holy Spirit all at the same time, a sort of two-for-one deal, and that relieved a lot of pressure. You could listen to the radio and be reassured about this fact:

Born'd again, free from si-in-in,
I' m happy ni-ight and day.
Make me shout, there's no dou-ou-oubt,
I know I'm born'd again.

Now that is a song to live by. You can get happy on that one.

But NO. Up in The County, it wasn't enough to be born'd again. I learned that it was not policy to be happy, because happiness depends on things that happen, whereas joy is deeper. It is inside, and doesn't depend at all on what happens. So we sang:

The sands of time are sinking,
The dawn of Heaven waits,
The summer morn I've sighed for
the fair, sweet morning awaits.
Dark, dark hath been the midnight,
but dayspring is at hand
and glory, glory dwelleth
in Immanuel's land.

Oh my goodness, how I missed Jimmy. Indeed, I was a timorous tadpole from Tennessee and in strange waters. At least back home I had one friend that was free of such gloomy constraints. When Jimmy got saved, it was more of the born'd again variety than the sands of time type. And besides, it wasn't allowable to have a radio at that school in The County, so I didn't have any reliable, external resources to nurture my faith.

In The County, born'd again didn't qualify. They didn't know about that option. They talked about obeying The Discipline and being faithful to the Jesus, which was one and the same thing. They would have Spiritual Renewal, where you could dedicate your life to God or, as the case may be, Rededicate Your Life. That was when your "All on the altar a sacrifice laid," and then you could take your turn at the microphone and announce that you were rededicated and now you have peacenjoy in your heart, like you never had before.

Peacenjoy. The concept was attractive, but it seemed to me to be as authentic as the claims of Smilin' Jack, the used car salesman. When they proclaimed peacenjoy, it sure didn't look like they had much of it. Maybe that would have ruined a ubiquitous principle if it showed. They looked about as pressured and as miserable as I felt during those religious olympics, and I didn't see a point of trying to get more of what I was trying to get shed of.

Now Mr. Smith, not our neighbor Mr. Smith, but the other one, he would get happy in church. It kind of scared me, and we wouldn't have allowed it in our church at all, but when he got the Spirit in his church, he would just stand up and scream out loud. Real loud. Everybody got a good chuckle out of it, and the preacher was gratified, and didn't miss a beat in the sermon. To me, that seemed a bit more in line with the peacenjoy frame of reference, but they saw things differently in The County.

Oh, boy, did they ever. They didn't believe in the Spirit like they did in Tennessee. In The County, the Spirit wasn't supposed to make you happy. It was supposed to convict you of sin. So if you had peace, that meant you had unknown sin, and if you enjoyed yourself, that meant you didn't have the Spirit. So the claims of peacenjoy somehow lacked authenticity, at least to me. It seemed to me that the Spirit was most helpful in convicting bishops, preachers, principals, and dorm supervisors of other people's sins. That is how that worked out. "I just have this feeling that somebody here has something they need to confess." They were big on wanting us to confess. If you got miserable enough and confessed to something generic, like pride in your life, in a contrite and abject enough manner, then you could join in the croaking choir, "Peacenjoy, peacenjoy, peacenjoy" and get those buggers off your back for a while.

I knew about peace and joy back in Tennessee, but not on those terms. It was just *different.* The whole environment just felt more healthier and life giving. Take for instance, when we would camp out in Mr. Smith's woods, not the other Mr. Smith, but our neighbor Mr. Smith, now that was a setting for *real* peace and joy. It doesn't get any better than lounging around the campfire, scratching, spitting, and telling lies, and then one of the Johnson boys, Cotton or Trey, or one of the others, would grab a burning stick out of the fire and yell out, "Far Tag!" That was a game we invented. Ever who had the stick was "It," and the person who got the burning end run up his butt would be the next It. Fire Tag got as active as a Baptist revival altar call at Jimmy's church, down there on Yarnell Road, us hooting and scampering. After a while it would be over and back to the fire again. Boys, now that there is a prime example of peace and joy. You could just feel the camaraderie. You didn't have to put words to it. You just flopped by the campfire and knew something very special was going on.

Spiritual Renewal in The County never approached that level of satisfaction.

I finally decided to part ways with The Discipline and related things when I learned that in The County, a girl needed to wear long sleeves, because elbows were the sexiest part of their body.

Say what?

I didn't know a lot about systems of knowing truth in those days, but something seemed just a bit out of kilter with that one. 1-1/4" covering bands could conceivably be Spirit ordained, but this one just flew in the face of all experience. I just knew something wasn't quite right with that line of thinking.

This I knew, because my adolescent juices worked overtime when Patti Lou moved in up the road. Patti Lou lived between my house and Jimmy's house. She had many fine attributes that not only spoke but also shouted, very fine and obvious, and me and Jimmy discussed them on occasion, but never ONCE did her elbows figure in the conversation. I, and Jimmy, too, would have liked to spend some special time with Patti, but her daddy was a big man, and we got the impression that he was sort of protective of her and, moreover, that he was not favorably impressed with us. We kept our distance. Oh, Patti, Patti, Patti, Patti. Do you know how we suffered because of you? And to this day, I can certify that it had nothing at all to do with her elbows. But I would have been glad to pat even one of them.

No, those ecclesiastical bullfrogs calling the shots in The County were off beam with that one. That I knew for sure. And if they missed such an easy one, what evidence was there that they were any better with other stuff that I was less sure about? I didn't need anybody messing with my mind, and the best defense was to get suspicious and cynical.

OK. So what. Who cares? So what if I grew up in a small pond, being Mennonite in Knoxville. I have no evidence that a larger pond in The County grew any better frogs. I guess when you get right down to it, everybody wants to believe that the best frogs come from their own pond.

"Born Again," as sung by the Louvin Brothers
"The Sands of Time are Sinking," Anne R. Cousins, 1857. Public Domain

Pleasures of Sin

According to modern thought, I should be embarrassed or at least ashamed for my old timey ways. I can't help it, however. It was just the way I was raised. O sure, I enjoy new and improved, but still long for old and predictable.

And when it comes to the Bible, well, it is clear that the Original Version is the best. I refer to the King James Version. You aren't supposed to read it silently. The KJV is meant to be read aloud, with the poetic statements rolling off the tongue, whirling through the air, echoing in heart for decades. I like the thee's and the thou's, the shalt nots, the haths, and giveths, and the real tongue twisters, like concupiscence. The great questions, like "Art thou in health, my brother?" whilst the beard is being grabbed and a sword is thrust between the fifth rib. And the exclamation: "Samson, the Philistines be upon thee!" That was a good one to roar out when your brother would overpower you. "Samson, the Philistines be upon thee!" and the strength of ten would come upon you and with the sword of the Lord and of Gideon you would vanquish the puny strength of your elder brother.

Now, Brother Jennings had his favorite phrases, too. He would preach about Mary and Martha, and how anguished they were at the death of their brother Lazarus. Mae-ree met Jesus on the road and said those eleven words, OOOOh-hh-hh, those eleven words, those eleven PRECIOUS words, "Lord-if-thou-hadst-been-here-my-brother-had-not-DIED." Yes, those eleven words, knuckles tapping on the pulpit to catch your attention, then reciting them off with the precision of a six-shooter, counting them on the fingers, punctuated with heartfelt tears on the "died." "O, sir, if you had only been here, my brother would still be alive" is supposed to be a new and better way. No sir. I don't buy it. It is more than eleven words, and it does not fit my image of Brother Jennings. That is not knuckle-rapping stuff. It just sounds foreign to my ears. It does not roll around satisfactorily in the ear.

Then there was a phrase that got preached about from time to time: The pleasures of sin for a season. What a wonderful collection of s's that slide across your consciousness and slip into your working memory. Sin was clearly bad, so they said, but here the Bible said, the pleasures of sin for a season. I liked the sound of that. It invited thought, and sort of encouraged a bit of dabbling for a spell.

Now let's get one thing clear right up front. Being as I grew up Mennonite in Knoxville, I didn't receive much encouragement for dabbling. In fact, it was downright frowned upon. Being caught, well, let's just say that punishment was swift and destruction was sure. But I surely considered the pleasures of sin for a season, and hoped that my season would hurry on up and get there, because I needed a bit of pleasure in my life. We weren't real big on pleasure in those days. Misery was supposed to be good for you; it built character. I didn't want character. I wanted pleasures. So I had to be inventive. My search inspired individual initiative, and I am happy to report that I found success now and again, and I am not sorry one little bit. I enjoyed it back then and relish the memories today.

One of my first escapades into forbidden territory had to do with an outhouse. Not an outbuilding - an outhouse, a Johnnie house, a privy. My boyhood pal Ralph had an outhouse in the field across from his house, the real, authentic version. Modern conveniences are great, and I believe in them, but it is not the same as visiting an outhouse.

For a kid, just getting used to a regular toilet has its own terrors. Your little bottom doesn't quite span the expanse of the seat, and there is always the fear of toppling over in backwards, head first. Then stuff that has been part of you for so long departs from you, and there are some feelings of loss associated with that. Then the awful whirling, gagging, sucking sounds when the flipper thing is flipped. The water swirls, and rises in a terrifying fashion, rising and rising and swirling before the tide ebbs. It could run over and sweep you far, far away. I tell you, that is scary stuff for a little kid. You didn't want to fall in and get pulled into the maelstrom of the potty. You would never get out again, gone forever, with nobody to notice your untimely departure. Plus, while you are sitting there, you can never tell if something will creep up and take a hunk out of your nether regions. It could, you know, and you would never know it was coming. There were stories of rats and snakes and crocodiles that swam up the toilet and grabbled little kids' dangling members. Going to the toilet for a little kid doesn't hold the fascination as it does for 80 year olds.

But that is peanuts compared to going to an outhouse. I tell you what. That is entering new territory of "terrors that stalk at noonday." Man, those outhouses have cracks in the wall, and you never know who would come up and paste their eye against the crack. And I seldom saw an adequate latch on the door. This is just for a start. I didn't even get to the fear of running a wood splinter into your privates, or the awful thought that there might really be something down there. A black widow spider sharpening its fangs, waiting for some tender flesh, a real rat, a convict hiding out – and the visual impact as you peered down into the hole made you think deep thoughts. And man, those holes were DRAFTY, and you just knew you would catch pneumonia of the bottom by sitting there too long, to say nothing of the real danger of losing things precious to you.

The outhouses I was familiar with were built for utility, not for style. Some leaned, some had rotted wood, and some had holes in the planking. The outhouse across from Ralph's house clearly was not designed by Frank Lloyd Wright. It was of the utilitarian school of architecture. And it was built on your standard East Tennessee field, fit only for raising shale and sage grass. Sage grass grows waist high and has nice fuzzy, hairy heads on it.

Ralph needed to go real bad. "I gotta go," he announced, and headed to the outhouse. Somehow I began thinking devious thoughts, and these thoughts ripened into action when I spotted a rotted hole in the back of the outhouse, positioned right under the depository inside. Quick as a wink, I plucked a nice handful of sage grass, with long stems and hairy heads, and waited just for the right amount of time. Then I snuck up behind, knelt down sort of like I was praying in church, and extended the stems in, in, in and up,up,up, swishing around very delicately.

Bingo! I knew it was mission accomplished when Ralph's scream rent asunder the tranquility of the countryside. Like Jesus Himself, Ralph ascended into the heavens. Or maybe it was like Elijah, riding the chariot of fire. I don't know for sure, as I didn't actually see it. I just imagined what happened based on the sound and other evidences. It was so gratifying. After the boards stopped their alternating concave and convex configurations, and silence resumed, I thought, well, that worked pretty good. Wonder if I can do that again. I waited very patiently, and once again, quietly, slowly, in, in, in, and up, up, up, swishing lightly from side to side. Again, like Jesus, Ralph was waiting to judge the quick and the dead. He was poised for action, bladder primed and ready, and when those hairy sage grass heads got in firing range, he cut loose with a torrential blast that is the envy of any male over 50. The heads of the sage grass got soaked and heavy. I didn't want to hold on anymore.

Eewww. Yuk. That was uncalled for. But it was pleasurable for a season. At least until old Ralph spoiled all the fun.

You see, it just doesn't work to preach about the pleasures of sin if you don't want me to go there, especially the good old timey version of pleasurable sinning on a seasonal basis.

Daddy Sang Bass

I guess a lot of people who don't know any better would sort of feel sorry for us, being as we grew up Mennonite in Knoxville. After all, there were lots of pleasurable things we weren't allowed to do, like watching television, smoking, cussing, public sports and mixed bathing. Well, for my part, and at this point in my life, I feel sorry for those folks who have to think that way, because they are just limited in their perspective in at least two ways. Number one, just because you aren't allowed to do something doesn't necessarily mean you don't go on ahead and do it anyhow and enjoy it, and number two, we created our own entertainment, and that was just fine, then and now.

For instance, my dad was an X-ray technician, and back in those days, X-ray film came wrapped in a folder of yellow paper. Boxes and boxes of yellow paper came home. It is amazing what you can do with an unlimited supply of yellow paper. Sometimes we used it to color on, and that was good. We explored the limits of yellow paper in aeronautical engineering. We learned that yellow paper was not stiff enough to make good airplanes. I liked best of all to create a control panel for a rocket ship and travel far beyond 1018 Connecticut Avenue to the far reaches of space. I can't imagine those early Mercury astronauts had more pleasure than I did. It just isn't possible, because they didn't make it out of Earth's orbit. I wasn't limited by normal rules of geo- and astrophysics. I had imagination, which was far more convenient to work with. I went beyond the sun, moon and stars, and came back, all in the same day. The yellow paper control panel never failed me.

Another thing we had going for us was good old-fashioned southern gospel music, with a nice tincture of blue grass. We would listen to it on the AM radio dial, on WIVK. That is the station that carried Mull's Singing Convention of the Air, with the Rev. J. Bazell Mull presiding, along with his wife, Mrs. Mull. Since J. Bazell was blind, he needed her to spin the record player and to turn off the microphone on him when he got to laughing too hard. Oh, how I loved that singing. The Chuck Wagon Gang and the rest of the groups. It just doesn't get any better than that.

Dad even had somebody put a special wire harness in the radio so we could record music from the radio to the tape recorder without having to use the microphone, which would pick up all the background noise. You would take a wire that had a 1/4" plug on one end and a set of alligator clips on the other, connect radio and tape deck, start the tape running and switch the knob on the front from "Play" to "Record." It was a brave thing to do to change that knob from "Play" to "Record." The consequences for leaving the knob on "Record" when you were done recording or recording over what you shouldn't were too horrible to contemplate. It was an act of bravery to record from the radio.

What with hearing that music on the radio, and over and over again on the tape recorder, that music became as much a part of us as okra and fried chicken. You learned about 4-part harmony, and how it could sound when somebody other than the Mennonite Hour singers would do it.

Naturally, you just had to sing it, and we did. We got one of those red Singspiration books that contained a lot of the Chuck Wagon Gang songs, and as we got older, we sang them together as a family. But before we got old enough, my parents sang in a quartet with Fred Dothan's parents. They were Janie Dothan's parents, also, but that didn't count because she was a girl and Fred was a lot more fun to be around.

Oh, it was so much fun to go over to Mary Elizabeth and Martin Dothan's house, over there in south Knoxville. The parents would sing, and while daddy sang bass, my brother and I learned new avenues in pushing the limits, thanks to Fred Dothan. He was brave when it came to dealing with his mother, much braver than I could ever be. If he got hungry, for instance, and wanted a slice of baloney, he would just take and sneak it out of the Frigidaire, hide behind the washing machine and eat it. Then he would call out, "Mom, can I have a piece of baloney?" You see what I mean? That was good thinking. After all, he asked for permission, and if Mary Elizabeth called back, "No!" there was nothing lost, because he already had it and couldn't put it back. He didn't seem to be bothered with excessive guilt, and I sort of admired him for that. I did not admire him for liberating a slice of baloney for his own self, and not for me – but on the other hand, that oversight spared me from moral culpability. I got the vicarious satisfaction without the burden of guilt.

Fred knew how to get along at school. He told us stuff that was very entertaining, about shop class and gym class. He made gym class sound interesting. There was this big curtain that divided the gym into two parts, the girls' side and the boys' side. They didn't have tennis shoes in those days, so they did gym in stocking feet. Fred said the boys would go sliding backward in the curtain when coach wasn't watching, so their rear ends would push the curtain over on the girls' side. But one of the coaches on the girls' side got wise to this and waited for a protruding rear end with a bolo paddle.

We made agreements with Fred, like as if we were ever at his house before he got home from school, we could go to the top of the hill above his house and make a fire, and send smoke signals, and he could see them at school and then he could try to get home sooner. I did wonder how he would see the signals from inside his school, but didn't want to spoil the moment with needless conjecture.

I enjoyed those trips to Fred Dothan's house. It was such an adventure to cross over the Tennessee River and turn left, meandering through the hills of south Knoxville. It took forever to get there, even after we got the 1955 Chevy. Fred Dothan's house sat up on the side of a hill, and you could spy the gable end through the trees long before you got there. We would stand up in the back seat, trying to be the first to see Fred Dothan's house, leaning forward, straining and quivering with anticipation, hoping to be the first to yell out, "I see it!" Since I would often forget the position of my mouth in relationship to my father's right ear, he did not always share in my enthusiasm about being the first to see the house. I gathered that in part by his facial expressions, but mostly by his verbal responses that did not carry many features of benediction. I couldn't help myself - I was just so eager to be first. How could I help it if he stuck his ear right where I wanted to shout? I was so eager to get there, and catching the first sight made it so I could endure the rest of the trip. It was great to play around, swaddled and secure in the sound of our parents' singing, the 4-part a-capella singing, done just for the fun of it. They too made their own entertainment.

There was some element of risk, going to Fred Dothan's house, because the driveway was so horribly steep, and there was once this guy who didn't set his parking brake and his car rolled down the driveway, across the road, and down in the ravine on the other side. They had to get a tow truck out to winch it out. I was concerned that I might fall on the driveway and roll all the way down, across the road, and into the ravine on the other side, and nobody would miss me for weeks, and when they found me I would be just a skeleton. And then you never knew if Fred Dothan would get caught doing something sneaky, and if we would get caught up in corporal punishment because we should have known better even though we didn't start anything or even do very much in terms of aiding or abetting.

But there was enjoyment all around, because the kids roamed, and the parents sang. And those songs sank deep into my soul, even when I wasn't exactly listening to it. And that is the way it is supposed to be when you grow up Mennonite in Knoxville.

Choosing Sides

My name is Ken. I prefer to be called Ken, even though my given name is Kenneth, and Kenneth carries a meaning of "handsome." Ken suits me just fine, because it is short and to the point, three letters and one syllable – two, depending on who is saying it. My friends call me Ken, and every time I mention how much I hated being called Kenny, I gain a whole new crop of enemies. One should never reveal their un-preferred name. For some dumb reason, folks find amusement in calling you exactly what you just got done saying please don't. I got called Kenny while growing up Mennonite in Knoxville, back in the days when it was important to me what my preferred name was.

Part of the reason I appreciate a monosyllabic name is that it sort of invites just a casual glance. Not exactly a dismissive look, but one that doesn't linger long enough to uncover all my inadequacies. And in the world I populated in Knoxville, it seemed that my storehouse of inadequacies was close to inexhaustible. Just so many of them, on so many fronts, and I got reminded of them in all sorts of ways in school, especially with anything concerning physical dexterity, academic achievement, social graces, or athletic accomplishment. And in all those arenas, I was called Kenny. Oh, how I hated to be called Kenny.

It wasn't so bad until I got in 6th grade. In the first five grades, I attended Lonsdale Elementary School, and there we played kickball. I could do kickball fairly well, and if you had friends, you would get picked to be on a team. Then there would be other kinds of games that didn't have teams, exactly, and that was better yet.

All that changed in 6th grade when we moved out to Concord, west of Knoxville, and I enrolled in Ball Camp Elementary School. There, what mattered most was if you could play softball. And I couldn't. Not for lack of desire, but for lack of any kind of skill whatsoever in hitting, running, catching, or throwing. Those deficits rule out being a prized team member. And no matter how much you want to do better, if you don't have the right stuff, well, you are simply out of luck.

One learns quickly about these things when one plays softball in 6th grade at Ball Camp. "Easy out," they would call out when I came up to bat. "Hey, boys, better back up," they would shout, and then the whole outfield would turn around and back up so they all clustered in the infield. And that was before I even got to swing the bat. Normally, it took a maximum of three pitches to get me out, being as I would still be swinging the bat while the catcher was heaving the ball back to the pitcher.

And then, when our side was in the field, I would lurk along the foul line in right field, praying fervently and earnestly, "Please, please, please, Dear God, don't let a ball come my way. And if it does, send somebody over real quick to catch it." I couldn't depend on those prayers being answered, and the proof of that was the number of times my glasses got broken because the ball hit me in the face rather than landing in my glove, or if I did get a glove on it, invariably my left thumb would get sprained so badly I was sure it was broken. "Oh, no, broke my thumb," I would moan in mortal agony. I hated softball.

Bad as playing softball was, choosing sides was even worse. I never got to be a captain, for obvious reasons. Generally it was people like Nancy Ann, Barbara, or Ralph, people like that who got to be captain and would take turns choosing up sides. If it was a good day, maybe Jimmy got to be captain, and then maybe, just maybe, I might get to be chosen somewhere down around ninth or tenth choice instead of last. The worst possible time was when it was just me and two girls left over, and neither captain wanted any of us. The job had to be completed, and there was dissention among the ranks about what to do with the leftovers. "Oh well," one captain finally announced to the other. "If you take the two girls, I guess I will take Kenny." Everybody just had to be on one side or the other, regardless of how painful it was.

Now do you understand a bit more why I hate to be called Kenny? And why I cringe whenever there is an expectation of my participation in sports? Or when there is a hint of choosing sides?

I hate it when choosing up sides is going on. A couple of somebodies will be left over, will be last, granted admission only reluctantly, and will cringe on the sidelines hoping they won't make their side lose the game.

Growing up Mennonite in Knoxville, I got the notion that we were supposed to be a chosen people, a royal priesthood, and something rather special. And because of that, we needed to make sure we remained separated from the world around us. Well, in church that sounds just fine, but it is not very sustaining when you can't play softball and it is time to choose sides. I was separated all right, a peculiar person, and I detected no virtue in being separated from my peers either by dogma or generalized clumsiness. Don't ever recall feeling like I was in a royal priesthood, or chosen in any kind of good way.

Furthermore, I loathe, detest, and utterly despise the spiritualized version of choosing sides for softball. "Hmm, Brother X is sound, but Brother Y is not sound. I have a few concerns about Brother Z. But Brother C – he is deliberately trying to lead people astray." You can be on our team, you cannot. I serve notice here and now, I will not play in that game, thank you very much. I have watched that brother game being played, hoping and praying, "Please, please, please, Dear God, don't let that ball come my way."

Today my friends call me Ken. I prefer it that way. A couple of rather special people call me Uncle Kenny, and I can do more than just tolerate it. I luxuriate in it because I was chosen to be on their first squad and I like it that way.

Canvassing

I guess my reward will just have to wait until I get to heaven, because I don't believe I got any of it here in this present life. It all had to do with Bible School and stuff like that. Bible School was fun, what with all the singing and activities, but what made it less enjoyable was what happened before Bible School started.

You see, it was like this. We wanted to have a big Bible School. We wanted our friends and neighbors to come. We thought it would be good for them to come to Bible School, and I guess it really was. I didn't think too much about it until I got old enough to be given detestable assignments, like inviting our neighbors to come along to Bible School. I don't recall any of us jumping up and down for the chance to go canvassing for Bible School. Somebody else was supposed to do that, and I felt so guilty for not having more success at even wanting to go canvassing. But at least I tried, in sort of a half-hearted sort of way.

It made me think of being a salesman of the door-to-door variety. I had tried that already, following in the footsteps of my older brother. Knocking on doors, and asking, "Do you want to buy any Cloverine Salve? It really works." I am sure there are many prosperous businessmen who started out in similar fashion, but I couldn't get anybody interested in buying a tin of salve, even for 35 cents. I knew it was nothing more than petroleum jelly, because that is what it said on the tin, if you read the small print on the side. But there were premiums if you managed to sell ten tubes of Cloverine Salve, ten tins per tube. Sounded real good, but alas, I couldn't even sell one tin, let alone ten tubes. It sort of clarified that I was not cut out to be a salesman.

So when it came to trying to sell people on the idea of Bible School, I didn't have a whole lot of confidence in any positive outcomes, at least in terms of convincing anybody that they would be welcome and wouldn't they like to come, please? That is not to say there weren't outcomes, because there were. Old Mr. Cash, down there close to Ball Camp Elementary School, he had this mean kick dog that I knew about, but since I was on a sacred mission, I thought I would be protected. Huh, baloney. That old dog came out snarling and snapping and sank its yellow fangs into my ankle. So instead of inviting him and his family to Bible School, I lectured him about tying up his dog if he knew what was good for him and his dog. I forgot something pretty important in human relations. In East Tennessee, a man takes it personally if you say things about his dog. Don't ever recall seeing Mr. Cash at Bible School. I never liked him too much anyway because his dog bit me.

I didn't even ask any of my associates from school to come. Intuitively I knew that based on my social ranking, I had very little pull with the cool kids. None of them wanted to be associated with me very much. Maybe in the same classroom but certainly not in anything out of school. So I knew better than to invite them. We sang about Jesus wanting us for a sunbeam, but I knew that my light was rather faint and flickering in the eyes of the kids I wanted to be around. And Jimmy – well, I selfishly didn't invite him because what if he came and got saved? Then he wouldn't be nearly as fun to be with. I couldn't risk that.

But there were the Stuarts, living up the road just before you got to Jimmy's house. They were a hardscrabble family, and if anybody needed to go to Bible School, it was the Stuarts. There was Mr. Stuart, and I guess a Mrs. Stuart somewhere, Granny Stuart, Sharon Stuart, Randy Stuart and another half dozen or so of Stuarts running around. We knew the Stuart family, because they would walk down to our house to use the telephone from time to time, being as they didn't have one. Sometimes they would give us a dime for using the phone, sometimes not. It didn't matter. It was a pretty good walk for them, past a number of houses with telephones to get to our house.

Old Sharon Stuart was very adolescent, and Sis Smith declared she caused an accident there on Shaffer Road because of the way she was walking along. "That Sharon Stuart. She caused that assiden' a-walkin' like that. Driver was a-lookin' at her instead of lookin' at the road. That Sharon Stuart. Hit was her fault. Shouldn't of been a-walkin' like that." Sis had opinions about Sharon Stuart, and they weren't entirely positive.

Now, Mr. Stuart, he was about as scrawny as they come, lean of muscle, long on sinew, and leathery of face. His right arm was black and blue nearly up to the shoulder. I asked Mr. Stuart if the kids could come to Bible School. I mean I walked on his property, right up to his house, right to where he sat, and invited his kids to come to Bible School. "Bi-ba Schoo'!" he proclaimed. "Har har har. I got my own Bi-ba Schoo' up thar in the corn patch. That-air is whur my kids do Bi-ba Schoo'." He got some merriment out of the thought. He even invited me to come to his Bible School if Bible School was such a good idea. All at once I had mellow thoughts for his kids, including Sharon. Personally I knew I would prefer being in Bible School rather than in a corn patch on a hot summer day, especially if Mr. Stuart was in the same patch.

The kids and Granny Stuart sort of milled around, and I felt like I was in foreign territory. Granny Stuart quavered out, "Randy, you better git down from up thar, or I'll tear you apart." Randy was climbing around on a lumber pile and wasn't interested in stopping. "Randy, I mean it. I'll tear the skin offen your back." Her threats didn't have much effect, because she was so frail and worn down by ineffectual threats. I wasn't sure if Randy would qualify for our Bible School.

But I wanted to try again. I thought maybe we could talk about something other than Bible School since after all, we were neighbors. "Mr. Stuart, what ever happened to your arm? It is all black and blue." "Yar. Old cow did that. Got an apple in hits th'oat. Nearly choked hitself, getting all blowed up and everthang. Liked to chewed my arm off when I retched in to get it out."

Apples and cows. I knew about that. We had this Black Angus cow. We called her Black. Every time she got ahold of an apple, she wouldn't chew it properly. She would just swallow it whole, and get it stuck in her throat. She nearly died a couple of times until we got the vet there to run a tube down her throat to dislodge that apple. I couldn't imagine running my arm down her throat, because Black was not responsible for her behavior when she was choking. Once I was holding her head while mom was trying to run the garden hose down her throat until the vet got there. Black was slobbering and moaning and blowing up bigger and bigger, and I got my little finger in the wrong place. She ground down on my little finger with her back teeth and popped the fingernail right off, and split the other side wide open. After the vet got there, and Black was out of danger, then we could attend to my affliction. Naturally the first course of action was to douse the entire end of the finger in Watkins Liniment. It said right on the bottle, "Good for man or beast." My mother pointed that out to me. Maybe that is what it said on the bottle, but it sure didn't feel so good.

So you see, I thought we had something in common. We talked about those stupid cows eating apples and getting all blowed up and stuff like that. "Well, Mr. Stuart, whattaya say? Can your kids come on out to Bible School?" "Har har har." He had a good reason for why not, and since he thought of it all on his own, he said it again. "Naw naw naw. Naw, huh-uh. We'll just have our own Bi-ba Schoo' up thar in the corn patch. Har har har."

Dang. Even though I grew up Mennonite in Knoxville and knew better, and hoped God would forgive me, but I wished that old cow would of chewed his arm off right up to the shoulder.

I am sorry to report that I had no more success in getting people to come to Bible School than I did in selling Cloverine Salve. And I am not going canvassing no more.

100

Mother Looked

They say you should be careful what you ask for, because you might get it. I never quite understood that saying, because I actually wanted what I would ask for, and had few experiences with getting what I wanted. Not for lack of asking or dreaming, but fiscal realities or character development seemed to get in the way. For instance, I wanted an oxygen tank, a snorkel, fins, and other apparatus so I could go skin diving. This was when I was eight years old, and even to this day folks think this was funny. Wasn't funny to me one little bit, because I wanted to go skin diving real bad. Never got my oxygen tank, so how am I to know I would have regretted it?

Back in the days when I was growing up Mennonite in Knoxville, I should have been more open to learning from the experiences of others. The sad reality is that for me, at least, experience was not a good teacher, either experiences of my own or experiences of others. Maybe I should have caught on a bit sooner about the perils of getting what you want.

It all had to do with ice cream. My mother loved ice cream, and every once in a while we would get to go to the ice cream place and get a cone for ten cents. Then they came out with an extra-large size cone, where they would really pile it on for twenty-five cents. Now that was a treat. And making homemade ice cream was a very special occasion, being as we didn't have a traditional ice cream freezer. So having a party where we churned ice cream was just heavenly. Mother liked the ice cream extra hard, so we tried to make it just right for her. We would make sure she got the part of the ice cream nearest to the edge of the canister, where it froze the hardest.

Then one day it happened. A once in a lifetime sort of event. We got a call from Brother Hunter, the superintendent of the Knoxville Rescue Mission. My parents were involved in the work there, and once in a while there would be too much of something donated, and Brother Hunter would call various supporters to come and get it. I don't know why he called us that day. Maybe he knew Mother liked ice cream.

Mother said that I was to drive into Knoxville and get some ice cream from the Rescue Mission. She said that Brother Hunter needed to clean out a deep freeze to make room for something else. A deep freezer of ice cream? That sounded like a bonanza, one worth sharing. "Mother," I asked. "Shouldn't we call Violet and Beth and Katie and let them get some of it, too?" "Nah," Mother said. "They don't need to know about this." You will recall my mother liked ice cream.

So I headed in to Knoxville, wondering what flavors of ice cream would be available. I thought there might be a few half-gallon containers, and that we would eat a lot of ice cream that night.

"Brother Hunter," I announced. "I am here to get the ice cream." He looked at me a little bit, and said, "OK....." "Well," I clarified, "my mother sent me in to pick it up. You did call her, didn't you?" Brother Hunter said, "Well, yes, OK....come this way." He took me to a rack of deep freezes, and told me they needed to be emptied of the ice cream containers. Boxes and boxes of them. "All of them?" I asked in a quivery sort of voice. He assured me they all needed to go.

I mean to tell you what. It was a great big huge amount of boxes. I began filling the trunk of the Dodge Dart. It was packed tight full. Then I started in the back seat, filling up the floor wells, the back seat, piled against the front seat, up to the top of the seat. Still had another freezer to go. I started in the front seat. Filled up the floor well, filled up the right side and center of the bench seat. Had just enough room to sit in and drive, if I squoze up tight against the driver's side door. The car sat squat on its springs, like I was hauling moonshine.

I headed toward Concord fast as I could, kinda weaving around. That Dodge Dart did not have extra duty suspension, and only a slant-six engine. I had to take it

102

kinda careful on the curves, as there was delayed reaction in the steering and extracurricular leaning happening.

Drove in the lane to the house. Ran in the house and announced that I was home, and would Mother come out to see the ice cream. Mother came out. I opened the trunk. I opened the back doors. I opened the front doors. "I brought the ice cream you wanted to have."

Mother just looked.

"Mother," I implored. "What are we going to do with all this? Where are we going to put it? It will surely melt on us. I don't know what to do with this ice cream. It is too much for our deep freeze, isn't it?"

Mother just looked.

"Mother," I begged, close to tears. "We got to do something about this thing. This ice cream will melt! It won't stay froze for a long time. It is hot outside. Mother, can I call Violet and Beth and Katie? There is enough for them, too, and we would still have a lot left over."

Mother kind of shook herself a bit, like she had just had a temporary stroke. Her speech seemed affected. Her voice was tight and strained, and filled with reluctance. "Call them," she said. She may have said other words, like, "Forever more," or "Oh my goodness." I don't recall that part exactly, because I was working in crisis mode.

Like good Mennonite women everywhere, Violet, Beth, and Katie were quick to respond in our hour of need. They came quickly. Some of the ice cream went back to Knoxville, but in different freezers than Brother Hunter's at the Rescue Mission. We were filled to overflowing with ice cream for the next couple of years. We could eat ice cream whenever we wanted.

I don't recall any conversations, exactly, with my mother about this incident. She seemed reluctant to comment. It almost seemed that she didn't appreciate any reminders. I surmised this because I tried it on a few occasions, when I would ask, "Mamma, do you want me to go get some ice cream?" She never said anything

103

exactly in response. She would get as rigid as a bird dog on point and gaze silently off into the distance. Never got an answer. Mother just looked.

Visiting

You didn't have to call ahead to make an appointment, back in those days. Visiting was just something you did to be sociable. You would just drop by to say howdy, set for a spell, and then move along. It was polite to go visiting, and to make time for visitors. We used to visit Mart and Ruby Stoltzfus's house on a regular basis, especially when there was corn to do up. I was too little to help with the corn, so I could roam around and explore. Found a toy box that had a toy saw in it. Found a board to cut up. That saw was made to look at, not to cut, but I didn't know that. It took five visits before I made it through that board. There are benefits to repeat visits to the same place.

When we moved west of Knoxville, out to Concord, Mr. and Mrs. Kendell came to visit us, walking down to road to our house, carrying a brown paper bag. It had black eyed peas in it. They wanted to welcome us to the neighborhood; it was the neighborly thing to do. Black eyed peas are a symbol of good luck, especially when you ate black eyed peas and hog jowl on New Year's Day. I learned to love those black eyed peas and believe in them to this very day.

I learned that visiting is different in Pennsylvania when I moved here in 1976. Nobody came to visit me. I thought, "Well, maybe they don't know any better. I reckon I will go visit them." Hoo boy. Was I ever right. They really didn't know any better. They didn't understand visiting one little bit. I went and knocked on the neighbor's door, and said, "Howdy. I am your new neighbor. I just moved in. I want to get to know you." That unnerved them a whole lot. They acted all skittish. I stopped doing that when I went to one neighbor who was working in his garden. I walked up to him, very carefully, so as not to step on any of those wee little corn plants. I took a deep breath to say, "Howdy," but he growled first. "Don't step on the plants!" he demanded. Well, now, I thought, you are an uncivilized stinker, and I don't rightly much care about your attitude. I decided then and there that I wouldn't go visiting him anymore. Those folks weren't bad people, I guess. They were just ignorant, that's all. Clearly, they did not grow up Mennonite in Knoxville.

We took our visiting serious, young and old alike. Take like one Halloween night, when I was just a bit too old to go regular tricker treating. Me and Jimmy , couple of the Joiner boys, and a whole scad of boys decided to go visiting in a friendly sort of way. Just to drop by at various places for a bit and move on. We took along extra rolls of toilet paper so people would have fond memories of our time with them. We really did have good intentions. But we ran into trouble after walking a couple of miles.

There was this old jalopy that came sputtering by, and someone yelled out of the window: "Trey and all the rest of you are queers." Jimmy, he rose to the occasion and yelled back, "And so are you." Buddy, I tell you what. I wished he hadn't of done that. It wasn't long until the hair stood straight up on my head, because somebody slammed on the brakes, ground it into reverse, and started backing up real fast to where we once stood. I say, "once stood" because we didn't stay there very long. We scattered like a bevy of quail, and shot out in all directions. Me and Jimmy headed to the school house, climbed up a rain spout and hid quiet as death itself, up there on the flat roof, nearly losing control of our bowels for anxiety.

After about two eternities, some of us regrouped and continued our visitation program. As the night wore on, we got further and further away from home, without exactly meaning to. We just visited around, even though we had lost our toilet paper. We just did regular visiting, albeit a bit late in the evening. Frankly, we forgot about time. It finally dawned upon us around midnight that we were afoot, and miles from home, and needed to head back. Plus that jalopy was still out there somewheres. And we didn't want to walk past old Mr. Cash's house because of that beagle dog. "I don't think it is a good idea to walk home that way," I announced. "Old Mr. Cash's dog might come out and bite us on the leg." I knew about that old dog. So we had to take the long route home, down Hardin Valley Road.

What I didn't take into account was that I hadn't exactly asked permission to go roaming on Halloween night. It was just an opportunity that presented itself and I sort of fell into it without giving a whole lot of thought to what my dad called "The Implications." The Implications came to us in the form of a pickup truck coming towards us around 1:30 a.m. there on Hardin Valley Road. There was no other traffic. Just that slow moving pick up. Some of the guys scattered. Me and Jimmy were just too beat to run. Besides, Jimmy said, very soberly, "I think that is my Pop."

It was.

Jimmy's dad did not have many words. I gathered he had been out roaming a bit his own self, but not for purposes of visitation. Jimmy and me, we understood we were to get in the back of the pickup. We didn't have much to say to each other. I think Jimmy was just a wee bit nervous. Come to think of it, so was I. Especially when I gathered there had been telephone contact between my house and Jimmy's.

You know, there are times in life when the will to fight is just not there. It doesn't matter if you live or die. It is all the same. I had a moment like that as I snuck into the house, much too quiet for everybody to be asleep. The frozen chains of disapproval that rattled and clanked like Marley's ghost were abroad that night. I just walked into my parents' bedroom, broke the silence by announcing, "I'm home." Dad replied, with heavy tones, "Mother and I are very disappointed in you." And that dreadful silence resumed.

I wish I could report that I regret causing that disappointment. Of all the disappointment I could have caused, that episode has to be on the benign side of things. I was sort of used to causing disappointment all around, so the damage to my soul was not particularly terminal in this instance.

Actually, the whole evening was one of my more enjoyable times of visiting. At least until The Implications came.

Lead Him On, Old Devil

It was such a strain on my constitution growing up Mennonite in Knoxville. There isn't anything wrong with Knoxville, or Mennonites, or Mennonites in Knoxville. But you put my natural disposition in the mix, somehow the gears of the machine that propels one into responsible adulthood start grinding a bit. I think we need to be honest here. There was some grinding and growling as I went down that assembly line, both from the forces trying to shape me and from me not being exceptionally amenable to the form I was supposed to get to. Something about irresistible forces meeting immutable objects – that is sort of what it was like.

They preached about the potter making a pot out of a lump of clay and if it didn't turn out right, well, the pot would be destroyed. They didn't talk much about starting over again with the same lump of clay. I gathered it was serious business if you couldn't shape up right after a certain amount of energy was expended on you.

It wasn't that I wanted to be permanently bad. Deep in my heart I wanted to wind up on the good side of things, but it was just so hard to walk through such a strait gate and down such a narrow path. Looking at it from a cost/benefit analysis perspective, I had to wonder if it was worth it to work so hard to stifle my natural bent. Clearly, my natural bent was not acceptable, and it seemed just a matter of time until my lump of clay would be swept off the potter's wheel and flung to the ground.

I felt personally responsible for my sad state of affairs, knowing I was doomed for all eternity before I had had a chance to live ten years. But then I made a wonderful, life-changing discovery.

I learned that I was not really entirely responsible for my actions, because they told us the devil crept abroad upon the face of the earth like a lion, seeking whom he could devour, and would cause you to do things that were not proper. That was a real relief when I learned that truth. It wasn't me after all! It was the devil!

The devil is very strong, you know, and the devil will trip you up at any moment; try as you might to avoid it. This seemed to make sense to me.

Fighting the devil seemed to be a low yield strategy, because he would get you anyhow. Jesus was supposed to help you gain victory over the devil, and the Holy Spirit was supposed to be a helper, but they didn't seem to be as intent in doing their job as the devil was. So you see, I really couldn't be personally responsible for all the internal and external grinding and growling that went on.

Besides, older folks commented on the regrets they had, and I didn't have any yet that were worth mentioning out loud. I felt kindly left out again. I felt I needed to get on with the program. I had some lost time to make up for. But work at it as hard as I could, I still didn't rack up too many regrets. I wasn't creative enough to explore all the possibilities as a ten year old. I just hoped the world wouldn't run out of opportunities for regrets by the time I grew up. I knew I had caused no end of regrets for the character shaping machinery, but that didn't count in a personal way.

So I kept clanking along, accumulating a few more years while those around me gathered battle scars. And I guess the devil kept watch also.

One summer, when I was working at Saint Mary's hospital, there in Central Supply, I met these crusty old women that were at least 50 years old. They worked intently on their various tasks, like cleaning, testing, powdering, and disinfecting surgical gloves. Back in the day there didn't have those disposable gloves. I wasn't qualified to do gloves. They didn't want me in the glove room. They would run me out in a decisive manner. I was supposed to stick to my job, not theirs.

Part of my task was to run the distillery, where we made pure water and saline solution for surgical procedures, then I would put these racks and racks of liter jars in the autoclave and let heat and pressure do its work. It was isolated work, even though I tried to imagine what it would be like to run a real still up in the mountains and run moonshine. They did that stuff in my days.

In the meantime, those women were busy in the glove room, cleaning the gloves, blowing them up to test for holes, powdering them, folding them just so. Fan running to provide a bit of air circulation in the glove room. And then there was me, sneaking past the open door now and again, waiting for the right moment to slip in behind them very quietly, and at just the right moment, clapping my hands.

Now I would have felt badly if I had caused any permanent damage. The distress I caused was temporary and enjoyable, except for the one lady, a bit more outspoken than your typical southern belle, who thought I was out of line. She didn't have much of a sense of humor. That is what it was. She could yell, but had trouble smiling at certain times. One day, after she spasmed, I heard her murmur sort of loudly, for my benefit and others in the glove room, "Lead him on, Old Devil. Somebody is going to get hurt."

That spoke to me, somehow. I didn't want to get led to the point of hurt, but I didn't mind messing around the edges just a little bit. I did back off a bit for that evening, just in case. But, all in all, I didn't and still don't have many regrets.

I guess the question is still open if it is about time to heave me off the potter's wheel.

"He Don't Speak Good English"

We didn't call them characters back then, but that is what they were. We just called them a sight. "Law, he's a sight!" was the pronouncement made when somebody got acting too big for his britches. And there were a variety of ways of addressing the issue when someone was a sight. Sometimes just a comment recognizing what they were was enough, other times you could sort of admire and support them by kind of egging them on.

There was this old Tennessee State Trooper stationed west of Knoxville. Now he was a sight when it came to getting your driver's license. He had a reputation of being mean and causing people to fail the driving portion of the test. He was downright nasty about it. I don't think he enjoyed giving driver's tests. Probably he had to give driver's tests when he didn't give out enough speeding tickets. That is how that worked. When I went in the first time to get my driver's license, Officer Ward was there being his own self. Some old boy, with solemn and earnest tones said, "One-a these days, somebuddy is a-gonna shoot him." I felt sort of chilly about that, knowing that there wasn't much dividing thought from action in that territory, and this despite the fact that there wasn't much future in shooting the law.

In fact there was a song about shooting the law, where the judge says, "Son, I don't mean to be rough, but this business of shooting deputy sheriffs has got to cease." And the guy replies, "You got a pint there, jedge." The song ends on a hopeful note, however: "Ninety-nine years on the old rock pile. It could have been worse. It could have been life."

I don't know if it was just coincidental, but I never heard anything about Officer Ward after that encounter in the police station.

But you take old Cas Walker. He was a sight. He was in to politics and grocery stores. You could stop, shop, save at the sign of the shears. Cas Walker's prices couldn't be beat, so he said. He was the forerunner of the

113

discount grocery stores. Part of his success as a grocer was being a sight. You could count on things happening when he was around, and he was always around. Things stayed sort of lively because of him. He sponsored these bluegrass shows on television and the radio, and they would sing:

> *Pick up your morning paper as it hits the street.*
> *Cas Walker's prices can't be beat.*
> *Take a sip of Blue Brand coffee and you'll call out for*
> *more.*
> *Do your grocery shopping at a Cas Walker's store.*

And old Cas would be there, sitting on the sidelines, saying, "Sing it again, boys." And they would. It was almost as good as a beer commercial.

Being as we were Mennonites growing up in Knoxville, we would try to stop, shop, save at the sign of the shears, especially if it was on our way to somewhere else. But my brother and I, being no respecter of person, and rather liking to stick a pin into the balloon of pomposity, sang our own version of Cas Walker's song:

> *Pick up your morning paper as it hits the street.*
> *Cas Walker's stores stink like his feet.*
> *Take a sip of Blue Brand coffee and you'll fall to the floor.*
> *Do your grocery shopping at some other store.*

I don't think there are any statistics that would indicate that we negatively affected Cas Walker's fortunes in any way, but we thought we were very smart, clever beyond all measure. I still believe we were creative in our disrespect for a cultural icon of Knox County.

Old Cas Walker was surely full of himself, and let the excess flow into the environment of Knoxville. He sat on City Council, and it was interesting to listen to the debates and vote calls on the radio. You could always count on fireworks when Cas Walker gave a speech. He gave a speech on every possible occasion. Even when

114

only an "Aye" or a "Nay" was called for. Just uttering one word hemmed him in way too much. The briefest he could be on a call for a vote, before he was gaveled into silence, would be something like: "Well, I'd like to say that I vote "Nay.'" He mostly voted, "Nay."

He was a man of deep convictions, and genuinely felt he was highly qualified to fulfill his part of the universal plan for humanity. He could come pretty close to convincing the citizens of Knox County of his greatness, especially when it was election time. One year, his election plank against his opponent was, "He don't speak good English like I do."

Law, he was a sight. You just have to give it to a fellow like that. That is not the kind of man you want to mess with.

Last I heard of Cas Walker was from an article in the Knoxville News Sentinel. It seems there was this woman who was suing him over an argument they had in one of his stores. Cas Walker didn't much believe in the modern day version of Customer Service. He did not believe the customer was always right, on account of the allegation that he knocked her to the ground and drug her out of the store by the hair of her head. He got some publicity out of that.

I don't know if Officer Ward was called in to the matter. Just think of it: Cas Walker, City Councilman, grocer, and entrepreneur, against Officer Ward and the majesty of the Tennessee State Troopers. I doubt either would have spoke good English. The encounter would have been likely only two shades less intense than a bunch of Mennonites debating things of importance, like versions of the Bible or the Second Coming.

Law, it's a sight.

Given to Hospitality

Thanksgiving Day was quite an event for us, back when I was growing up Mennonite in Knoxville. Of course we had a huge Thanksgiving meal, but we didn't have any family in the whole state of Tennessee to eat or visit with, so it was kind of hard to be hospitable on Thanksgiving Day. And naturally we didn't have any television to watch any football games on Thanksgiving Day. I guess part of it was we didn't know or care much about football, as that was a worldly pursuit. The other part was I doubt they even televised football games in those days. But even if they did, it didn't matter because we didn't believe in either television or football, so what's the use.

We went to church on Thanksgiving Day, because that was the proper thing to do, and would sing "Praise to God Immortal Praise," and "Come Ye Thankful People Come." Being as we sang that second one only once a year we didn't get the harmony down very good, but our hearts were in the right place.

The worst part of going to church on Thanksgiving Day, besides trying to sing "Come Ye Thankful People Come," was the yearly ritual of having to say out loud what you were thankful for. Brother Good, bless his heart, was a joyful man, and wanted us to be joyful also. He just didn't catch on that he was fighting a losing battle on that point. He would make us go, row by row, person by person, and state what you were thankful for. Now that was highly uncalled for, especially when Matt would say, every year, regular as clockwork, "For blessings too manifold to mention." He could get by with that sort of generic thing and the rest of would be stuck with having to be specific with our thanksgiving, and mumble out something like parents, or, living in a land where you can worship as you please. Adults could come up with stuff, like healthy children and the blessings of salvation, but man, it was a real chore for a kid to be thankful under pressure.

117

Now what I didn't know was the part that natural hospitality played in East Tennessee, and not just on Thanksgiving Day. I mean, hospitality was just the way things ran back in those days. "Come awn in and set by the far'" was a genuine invitation, and you didn't turn that down very lightly unless you had to get on home to feed the dogs or something like that. You would at least sit on the porch and visit for a spell and if you went inside the house, you would set by the fire and visit about all manner things. And of course you had to eat or drink something while you were there. It was just the proper thing to do.

"Why don't you come on over and eat supper with us?" was a way of being friendly. You weren't really expected to eat supper. The correct response was to say, "Naw, I cain't really do that. I got to get on over to the house." Sometimes the invitation would get more insistent, and you had to be creative about it to keep good relations, especially if you were unsure about the meal that was proffered.

And that was my situation one Thanksgiving Day. We had gone to church, and I was dutifully thankful, and ate a great big huge Thanksgiving meal, made by my mother. As usual, I ate way too much, and my tummy was stretched tight as the belly of a blood sucking tick on the ear of a foxhound. I needed a bit of exercise, so I went over to visit the Smiths. Crawled through the bob war fence, staggered past the sweet gum tree, past Mr. Smith's hog pen, and flopped down on the porch to let things digest. It was 3:00 in the afternoon, so I thought I was safe from any food invitation. Besides, I was constitutionally ill prepared to eat one more bite of anything, for fear of suffering dire consequences.

But Sis came out and said, "Come on in and eat turkey with us." "Naw," I said. "I done already ate. I couldn't hold one other bite." She wouldn't take "No" for an answer. Louise, she came on out, and when she spoke, you got a bit uneasy. She was large of frame, and

118

well filled out. One breast was three times the size of the other, and that lent authority to her demands.

"Come on in here, Kenny, and eat with us." Honest, I tried to say it would not be good for me to do this. Neither one of them seemed to understand very well. "I cooked up this turkey, and I want you to have a plate of it." I went into the kitchen and saw that turkey. My stomach had an epileptic seizure. That turkey was cut up into squares, skin and all, with about a half-inch of fat between the skin and the meat.

Now I don't have anything against turkey, even on Thanksgiving Day. But turkey roasted on a cookie sheet in square blocks and not even brown on top was a bit too much for me in the delicate state I was in. Besides, I had a sneaking suspicion I had more than a casual acquaintance with that particular bird. One of their turkeys had misbehaved that fall, and ate up the corn that Sis was using to pen up some chicken. "Dumb old turkey et up all my carn," Sis wailed in a tone that was meaningful as to the longevity of that tom.

So there I was, weighing visceral civil war on the one hand, and politeness on the other hand. I knew I would suffer, no matter what decision I made. Actually, the decision was made for me. Quick as a wink, several squares of that turkey, and green beans cooked for 24 straight hours, potatoes, and pie – the full nine yards was set before me.

Being as I was my parents' son, there was only one course to take. That was to eat, and eat it all, and don't leave one tiny scrap on the plate, not even a glob of turkey fat big enough to grease the axle of a railroad train car. Oh, my, my, my. The Smiths were given to hospitality big time. And perforce, I gave in to hospitality.

I am happy to report, I think, that I did eat that plate of food. I am not happy to report that I did not linger too long to visit. Actually, other needs were pressing upon me. Visions of turkey fat floated before my eyes, and no amount of swallowing could get the picture lower than my throat. I made some sort of statement about not

119

really being able to stay, as I had to get on over to the house. I am not sure if I said thank you for the good meal. If I had, I would have lied two times over because I was not thankful and it was not good. I never did like turkey fat. Still don't. Waugh.

It was not a happy Thanksgiving Day for me, not one little bit. I did manage to hold my load past the porch, and out to the far end of the hog pen. Then my soul nearly departed from my body as I retched and heaved two Thanksgiving dinners into the hog pen. I heaved until I was nearly cross-eyed with agony, and all the strength left my legs. There I was, drooped over the hog pen fence, droopy as Raggedy Andy, not sure how much of me was dangling inside the fence or outside the fence, not even caring if one of those cob-rollers would come over and grunt at me. I just wanted to die. Every time I thought I was done, Satan would cause me to think, "Turkey Fat," and there would be another load fired up from the abdominal howitzer.

Oh how I suffered, all on account of hospitality. But I guess it was sort of worth it, being as the Smiths had the blessings of being given to hospitality on Thanksgiving Day. As for me, I hope I never again see a turkey semi-cooked that way. Ever.

"I Ain't Skeered"

Back when I was growing up Mennonite in Knoxville, we had lots of things to be afraid of. Take Curtis, for example. Otis had a pair of hedge clippers, and he walked the streets looking for hedges to clip, I guess. Now, hedge clippers are big and sharp, and make a squitch-kind of sound. Otis would make the clippers squitch and mutter, "I'm-a gonna cut off ye haid" whenever we would follow him around. I don't think he liked kids very much. He interested me a lot, and I sort of looked forward to him coming around, just to see if he had a change of heart, but also sort of hoping he hadn't. I thought maybe he had something else in mind he wanted to cut off, since a clippers would have trouble cutting off a head. The alternatives were too horrible to contemplate very long, but despite my best efforts, it seemed like his threats occupied my mind a lot. But it was still sort of an awful thrill, a horrible fascination, when he would mutter and squitch the hedge clippers.

I guess a lot of folks specialized in horrible fascinations, as we got to hear about that a lot. We learned about black widow spiders and poisonous snakes, and how they were just waiting to get you if you were in the wrong place. They were evil. Worse yet were those great big huge yellow spiders, those garden spiders. They were so big, about the size of a dinner plate, and they were not only poisonous, but deliberate about their intentions. These spiders knew how to write, and if ever they saw your teeth, they would write your name in their web in spider writing as a reminder to sneak in your bedroom at night to bite you.

This is true. Everybody knew that. Roger Benson said so, and Roger Benson knew about these things. He lived next door and was born a full-blooded Indian, and had to stay indoors for seven years in order to turn into a white man, and that proved that he had special wisdom about things.

It was sort of thrilling to be scared, but you weren't supposed to show it very much. Being a scaredy-cat was being a sissy, and sissies didn't thrive in Knoxville, even if they were Mennonite. No sir. No sir-ee, you had to be tough, even though that went against all theological precepts and teaching, being as we were supposed to be meek and submissive and all that stuff. Problem was, meekness and submissiveness don't lead to manliness, East Tennessee style. You had to get tough, or at least pretend you were tough. Only catch was, you had to sort of be tough to act tough and as Mennonites in Knoxville, we didn't believe in toughness. You were supposed to repent if you were tough. That was being ungodly, like the sinners next door.

But that writing spider was still there, just waiting to write down your name for a nocturnal visit. You could never tell where one would be, and it was such an effort to walk around with your lips tightly compressed. Soon as you forgot - bam - there you would run your face right into a writing spider web, with your mouth wide open. When you recoiled in disgust and horror, sure as shooting, there would be that spider, with your name written down.

This was serious stuff.

Spiritual heritage notwithstanding, something needed to be done about this situation. When religion doesn't have an answer, you need to drink from other wells. Roger Benson and them had a solution to this spider-induced frenzy. The best way of dealing with this is to dare that old spider, to challenge it. You just knew that it was writing down your name, and the consequences of it seeing your teeth were just dreadful, that solitary bite in the middle of the night. So what you did was walk up to the spider web, deliberately bare your teeth and say, *"Look! I ain't skeered!"*

You would dare that spider to do its worst. Go ahead! Look at my teeth! Write my name down! See if I care! You could quake on the inside, but you would glare and dare on the outside. And contrary to what they said in church, it wasn't what was inside that mattered. You had to get over that stuff. It was what was on the outside that really counted. If you could say it often enough, you would eventually sort of believe it.

Daring that spider was the developmental equivalent of induction into the armed services. It meant you were now a member of the select, the few, the proud, the initiated. You looked death in the face, and crossed over the gulf between boys and men. No passive acceptance of God's will, no fatalistic acquiescence here. To heck with spiders and their devious ways. Bring it on! Just try me. You bite me, you die. I will poison you my own self.

I am so grateful to my neighborhood mentors who ushered me into manhood, helping me to manage the terror that comes by night and the destruction that wastes at noonday. You just pull yourself together, look the agent of fear full in the face and yell, "I ain't a-skeered of YOU."

So come on, you traveling evangelists, you merchants of misery with your charts of the end times and cheerful promises of sinners burning in hell-fire for ever and ever, praise Jesus. Try to intimidate me now, you mournful ministers and bishops of the baleful gaze. I have had enough of your sticky strands and cryptic writing. Bring it on if you have to. Just know I am not a little boy anymore. I've said it once and I'll say it again until I believe it: "I ain't a-skeered-a you."

Generational Misadventure

There is a verse somewhere in the Bible that I used to hear about back when I was growing up Mennonite in Knoxville, and strictly speaking, that verse did not bring a whole lot of to comfort to me. It had to do with the sins of the fathers being visited upon their children unto the third and fourth generation. Didn't seem fair to me at all. And for some dumb reason, I sort of took that verse to mean I was supposed to behave myself in a proper kind of way right now, because if I didn't, there would be consequences. Someday I likely would be a father, and what I did now would cause untold misery for my children, grandchildren, great-grandchildren, and even my great-great grandchildren. This was a heavy burden to bear as a child. Four generations following me would wind up as drunkards, sluggards, gluttons, liars, thievers, convicts, and homeless all because I wanted to learn a little creative cussing, for example. It seemed out of balance, rather excessive, if you ask me.

But looking at it from the other direction, as a child, I did have to ponder on this from time to time. I mean, really. Whenever I was bad, I was the one who got the whipping. I had to do the suffering. Nobody ever went chasing after my daddy, granddaddy, great-granddaddy or my great-great granddaddy because I said "dern" to my friend Johnny there at 1018 Connecticut Avenue. I was the one who had to say, "I am sorry and will you forgive me," knowing that I would just die from embarrassment and humiliation, because Johnny didn't give a hoot if I said dern. Didn't matter to him. I would have consequences because of the implications if I didn't say I was sorry. Shoot. Where were my ancestors? Shouldn't they have to carry some of the heat? Where were they right when I needed them?

Waddn't fair. Seemed to me it ought to work in both directions. But it didn't. Puzzlement backwards and conjecture forwards.

Talk about puzzlement – take my Grandpa Yoder. He was something else. Unlike the rest of us, he was sort of a colorful figure, and cut a moderately wide swath throughout his life. He lived in Delaware most of the year, wintered in Florida, and visited us there in Tennessee once in a while on his travels south and north. Now he could say and do things that I could not. He could roar out things like: "How in the Name of All-That-Is-Holy" and he didn't get consequences. He could sit all spraddle-legged in the back seat of our '55 Chevy, crowding my brother and me into the far corner, lean over the front seat, complain about traveling with other people, and yell in my father's ear, "NO SIR. I AM NOT GOING TO BE CROWDED IN THAT CAR."

Two things here. Number one, and this is important. You don't lean over the back seat and yell in my father's ear. It is simply Not Done. But it was. By Grandpa. And that made it all right. Maybe that is why the heavens collapsed and all H-E-double-toothpick broke loose when I did it. Sins of the grandfathers, you know. Stands to reason. He gets by with it and I get the punishment for it.

And number two. He was the one doing the crowding his own self. Even a child could figure that one out. Again that didn't matter, being as it was beside the point. That is why me and my brother got whupped good and proper one time. It was due to Grandpa's crowding us in the back seat, only he wasn't there at all, but we had to pay the price.

It went like this. We were traveling to somewheres, and the road was long and the time in the back seat was tiresome. And to make it worse, I had to sit besides my brother in the back seat. Naturally, he took up more than his fair share of the space. I tried to remonstrate with him about this, but it was not well received, neither by my brother, nor by him who must be obeyed, there in the front seat driving the car. I recall some suggestions designed to improve matters in the back seat. If my memory is correct, one statement was crafted more as a directive than as a suggestion. My brother should of listened better. He should have taken heed. But no-oo-oo. After a brief interlude, he took and propped his leg way up high on the front seat. He pushed the limit on purpose just to see what he could get away with, sort of daring me to do something about it. I just knew he was going "Nanny nanny poo poo" in his miserable little mind, but he was acting awfully nonchalant about it, all spraddled out like that when he should have known better. When he DID know better.

Well. I ask you. What was I supposed to do? Grandpa Yoder wouldn't tolerate being crowded in the car, so why should I? I am not ashamed to say that I took matters into my own hands, so to speak. I reached up and pinched him in a tender spot. He made far too much of a deal out of it. He screamed like a sissy girl. It really wasn't all that big of a deal according to my lights.

But it was to someone else, as I gathered in short order. Instead of the car following the curve of the road, it went sort of straight and stopped on the shoulder. There was a fearsome silence in the car, front seat and back. The front door opened. The back of the front seat flew forward. Two boys went unwillingly outside the car, where we took in deep breaths of fresh air interspersed with heart-rending wails. These wails, must I mention, were a result of our nether regions being set on fire, as it were, from vigorous applications. No words were spoken. It was all action and no talk. Two boys went back into the car, the front seat went back upright, and the car completed the curve in the proper manner.

The outrage of it all was just too much for human endurance. What happened was simply unjust, unfair, unreasonable, and unnecessary. Naturally these thoughts remained unspoken, but there were a few residual sobs, sniffles, and whimpers.

There was a comment from the front seat. It did not communicate much in the way of understanding that Grandpa Yoder really was at fault here, if you really want to get right down to it. This whole misadventure was generationally driven, as anybody could clearly see. There was no recognition of this in any way, shape or form, in spite of the fact of Bible based teaching on this topic. What was said went something like this: "If you don't get quiet, I will give you something to cry about."

Huh? That happened already, don't you know. I mean to tell you what. I didn't want any more apples out of that bushel. But when your entire physical plant is convulsing with wave upon wave of pain, and you dare not make a noise in response - oh my goodness gracious. The agony ascended to throat level, and needed to be conquered there. One needed to choke it down, purse the lips, blow out the cheeks. Nearly got a aneurysm from it all. Almost bugged my eyeballs out. Probably came close to a serious nosebleed. Just about went permanently cross-eyed, all in an effort to be quiet.

And, who, may I ask, Biblically speaking, was responsible for this? And just why couldn't the punishment be retroactive? I would have been just as happy if my great-great granddaddy got his rear end polished, because after all, he started it.

"Who Dat?"

In spite of what you may think it was like growing up Mennonite in Knoxville, there were moments of merriment. We were not totally unaware of the concept of humor, because vestiges of it would creep through now and again. Grandpa Yoder had some adventures that were funny. He even created some adventures that were funny, and not because he wanted them or even thought they were funny, especially in the moment.

We loved those grandpa stories, being as he specialized in exaggerated reactions, kind of like a nervous cat. His feet were tender, and he didn't want anything other than socks and shoes touching the soles of his feet. That is what he wanted, but he didn't always get it, because one time, late at night on his way to the bathroom, he by accident stepped on a squeaky toy left there by some unfortunate grandchild. Now being as I was not there, I cannot attest to what happened next, but rumor has it that grandpa reacted in his usual fashion. It is probably best to not go too deep into conjecture here. Surprises of that nature tend not to bring out the best of one's essential character.

Another funny thing was this joke we discovered that went something like this. In the middle of the night, somebody thought he was alone in the house, and heard a noise. He called out, "Who dat?" Person number two thought _he_ was alone in the house and responded, "Who dat?" And things got worse. The first guy yelled out, "Who dat say who dat when I say who dat?" Now that was funny, and bore repeated retellings.

It could have happened to Grandpa Yoder in a way. He too heard a noise in the middle of the night and went to find out what it was all about. He didn't believe in using electricity very much, or putting on his glasses or combing his hair when he went on these nocturnal peregrinations. He looked out the window. Couldn't see anything. Lit a match and held it above his head to see outside. "You know," he said, "there was this ugliest looking man with hair all over his head looking right back at me in the window." He was startled and we were amused.

There were times when I discovered myself in the mirror and fell into deep thoughts. Who was that boy in the mirror? Was it really me or was it somebody else? I couldn't figure it out very well if I were here or there, or both at the same time. What was the nature of reality here? It was a philosophical, existential moment, sort of worrisome, much beyond my ability to resolve.

So I just had to deal with it the best way that I could. Never did get that one figured out. Reality is such a messy concept, and at times sort of scary.

There was this time, just recently, where reality presented itself in sort of an ambiguous and alarming way, quite undesired. It had to do with plumbing problems in our house to the degree that the entire water had to be cut off for days upon end. That reality created other realities in the body odor department because, well, there was no water to take a shower. So I went to my neighbor's house and asked Cindy if I could take a shower there. "Sure," she said. We are all the time helping each other out. Cindy's daughter is now a high school senior but she used to be little. She is not so little now.

Being as we are good neighbors and all, I asked Katie if she wanted to take a shower with me. I meant it in a friendly kind of way. "Nah," Katie said. "Well," I said, "I really don't mind at all." "I take my shower in the morning," she replied. "Oh," I said. "That's OK. I can wait and come over in the morning." "Nuh-UHHHH!" she said, with conviction. Her mother just grinned. It was all very friendly.

I went on my lonesome way into the bathroom, shut and locked the door, stripped down and headed into the shower.

It was just awful. There was this hideous ugly man headed right towards me - full frontal nudity, and the sight was just too horrible to bear. I saw things I did not plan to see, and none of it was desirable. I did not yell, I did not lose bowel and bladder control, but it was a close call. And after sober reflection, I had to wonder why Cindy did not warn me of the full-length mirror on the bathroom door.

I do not enjoy having the mirror held up to me. There are some realities that one should not be confronted with until you are ready for it, and even then, never in isolation. You need a lot of emotional support to deal with some levels of exposure. I don't think it is an absolute requirement to grow up Mennonite in Knoxville to come to that insight, but it might help.

Heaven, and getting to heaven, was a big topic back when I was growing up Mennonite in Knoxville. Everybody had an opinion about what heaven was like, and how you got there. It was just assumed that heaven was out there somewheres else and you wanted to be there in the end. I guess that was a reasonable thought, being as hell was going to be a very awful place, what with the fire that never goes out and the undesirable elements there.

Now your generic Baptists - they had a pretty good handle on these matters. They knew exactly what heaven looked like. The streets were paved with pure gold that you could see right through. There was this beautiful lake, only it was made out of the purest crystal. That didn't make any sense to me at all because you would break your neck if you was to jump in to take a swim in it. And all you needed to do to get there was to get saved. Boom. That is all there is to it. They believed in Once-Saved-Always-Saved, you know, eternal security, which was sort of a comforting thought. Get saved, get that part over with, and you don't have to worry about it. You would get to go to heaven and have a wonderful mansion there on the corner of Glory Lane and Hallelujah Avenue and be neighbors with the popular saints.

Now the Presbyterians had a different arrangement. It wasn't real important to get saved. It was actually out of your hands. God figured out ahead of time who would make it and who wouldn't. You got elected, even before you had a chance to go up for nomination or to run for the position.

The actual dimensions of heaven were figured out - it would be a mile high, a mile wide, and a mile deep. There would be mansions all over the place, but room for only 144,000 people. I tried to figure this out. I thought there were more Baptists and Presbyterians than that. And anyways, those mansions would have to be piled up sort of like martin houses or laying hen cages to fit those places in the specified volume, and that wasn't attractive to me at all.

Now when it came to Mennonites and heaven, things were a bit more ambiguous. We didn't hold to Once-Saved-Always-Saved or predestination. All we had was hope, and that was mighty slim pickings in the middle of the night when you had to ponder your sins and your eternal destination. We believed in getting saved on sort of a temporary basis, because you could always backslide, and, well, there you go again. You had to hope you died when you were saved and not backslidden. That is what we hoped for.

Well, sir. I hoped and prayed about this thing. I got officially saved at least twice before I was ten years old. I got baptized. I got rededicated more times than I can remember. Honestly, I tried and tried to have my "all on the altar a sacrifice laid." One time I had hands laid upon me to get the Holy Spirit and this guy prayed in tongues over me. I hasten to add that this last part did not take place in Knoxville. We didn't believe in the Holy Spirit like that. None of this seemed to be very enduring when it came to certainty about heaven or getting there. After a while I decided not to worry so much about hope and figure things out for myself.

So I got to figuring this thing out. How did they know heaven was really like they said it was? And who said it had to be that way? How come the Presbyterians, Baptists, and preachers get to set the rules about everything, anyhow? What if I didn't want to be there if I would get hurt if I wanted to take a swim? I don't know about you, but walking on streets of transparent gold doesn't hold any attraction for me. I guess their notions about heaven are actually more of a collective hunch than anything else, because nobody really knows. I think people make things like that up out of poverty of experience. So. I have a pretty good idea my own self of what heaven will be like, because my family had our own mansion, over there in Sevier County, close to the Smoky

Mountains, and that is good enough for me as an eternal destiny.

It wasn't located on a fabulous intersection. Heck, it was out in the boonies, and didn't even have a road all the way up to it. No electricity, no running water, stone and mud fireplace and chimney, two burner coal-oil cook stove, a privy out back, and an endless supply of old Saturday Evening Posts from way back when. It was set on 15 acres of wooded land, with a creek running through it, and was just the perfect place to roam around. Once in a while we would encounter a snapping turtle down in the creek, and that added just the right amount of dangerous thrill, because if a snapping turtle bites you, they don't let go until it thunders.

Now that is my idea of heaven. I will have me this little cabin, wall papered with cardboard and newspaper. I will get water from the spring, and will have a long-handled dipper to dip out of a ten-quart galvanized bucket. I will drink straight from the dipper and the water will be so cold it will hurt your teeth. Me and my buddies will set on the front porch of an evening and we will pick and sing. Being as I will have a glorified body, I will be able to pick a mandolin better'n Bill Monroe and I will sing high tenor, so high the sound will come right out the top of my head.

When it gets dark, the stars will be so bright and so close you could almost reach out and grab a handful and squeeze them until star juice runs down your elbow. You will look out and see the light given off from a rotting stump. Your dog will be there, lying in front of the fireplace, and your cat will be curled up in your lap. We will set around the fire and tell stories. My cabin will be far removed from the intersection of Glory Land and Hallelujah Avenue, and even further from Victory Square, because there will be too many noisy people there who will disapprove for some reason or the other. I won't need to be next-door neighbors with Jesus and Saints Peter and Paul. That will not bother me one little old bit. They can come visit me once in a while if they feel up to it.

135

Likely they will need some quiet time from all those pesky people crowding around like a bunch of hungry hogs at the feeding trough.

When they come visiting, I will have black eye peas and cornbread, with homemade butter and sweet honey. Don't get too wild about this part, but I might even have me a jug if somebody wants a nip now and again. Being as it is heaven and all, the jug will likely have to contain Kool-Aid. I will try not to be too disappointed. My family and friends will be their perfect age and they will visit as much as they want to, any time they want to set by my fire. Likely there will be times where I will keep the jug behind the door when folks drop by, because of appearances.

And as to that crystal lake - well, in my part of heaven there will be a real lake where you can go swimming regular style. And when you get done swimming, you can have a picnic on real grass rather than on a terrace lumpy with jewels.

And I tell you what. That business of only 144,000 getting there. That is just stupidity. That thinking don't make any sense at all. Seems like that is designed to figure out ahead of time how many you can keep out. Who has to specialize in that business, anyhow?

OK. Some folks have their notions about heaven. I guess that is all right if you have limited imagination and insufficient enjoyment here on this earth. For me, I don't have to worry about it at all because I already know what it will be like. I've experienced it here on this earth already, and it will just be more of it on the other side. And if someone tries to tell me that my mansion doesn't fit in their hunch of heaven, well, buddy, don't go messing with me about that stuff. Tell you what. If you don't like my version of heaven, you can just go and try out the other place.

Terror by Night

It was sort of unauthorized, and I guess that is why it was so enjoyable, that time when me and my brother, Jimmy, and a bunch of neighbor boys went camping up in Mr. Smith's woods. When I say unauthorized, that is exactly what I mean. We sort of had permission, but not in great detail. We left a lot out when we asked permission to go camping. Mr. Smith said it was OK, but he didn't want us to build a fire and burn his woods down. We promised we wouldn't burn the woods down, sort of shocked that he thought we would want to do that. And when you come right down to it, I doubt my parents had many of the details, or else they would have had a few reservations. We didn't want them to know a lot of details. Details had a way of derailing a lot of fun. Even though I was a Mennonite growing up in Knoxville, I still wanted to go camping with the neighborhood boys once in a while.

So we went camping up in Mr. Smith's woods. Mr. Smith's woods was a great place to explore. It had three main ridges and hollows. In one of the hollows was Mr. Smith's bone yard. That is where he would drag his dead cows, or mules or other animals, and in the daytime you could explore the bones and skulls and be brave. But at nighttime you didn't know what would be stirring in amongst the bones. At the head of the first hollow was this rotten stump where they said Mr. Johnson lived after his wife kicked him out. And then there was this hole dug in the side of one of the ridges where we thought people dug for gold one time. Maybe they stopped digging that hole because they got caught digging for gold and somebody killed them for the claim.

But at nighttime, you could never tell what might be creeping around. Mr. Smith's mules and his horse roamed the woods. There were noises that we tried to ignore, because we couldn't look scared in front of the other guys. It became real necessary to build a fire, and build it up pretty good so we could see out though the trees, but that had its disadvantages because at the edge of the light was still the dark, and the shadows would flicker around a bit, increasing a generalized sense of uneasiness. When you push back the boundaries of darkness, it increases the fear potential because there are so many more things to sort of half see.

I figured we ought to lay down and go to sleep, because if you are asleep you won't know if something is coming to get you. I had seen that picture of this guy sleeping in a desert, and there was this lion standing behind him. That picture scared me a lot, but the guy in the picture wasn't bothered because he didn't know that lion was there, pondering if he wanted to eat the guy or protect him. It wasn't clear what he ought to do next. That picture invited speculation about things. We had already put a long length of rope on the ground around our sleeping area, because everybody knows snakes won't cross over a rope. We had that department covered pretty good. But it wouldn't keep the spirits away, and they would come to vex you if you weren't careful. And it wouldn't keep vile characters away, and we had some of them in our territory.

The other guys got to telling stories, ghost stories and other scary stories. I didn't believe in ghosts very much, but it doesn't pay to be disrespectful about these things when you are in the middle of Mr. Smith's woods late at night. I mean, you can't really be sure there aren't ghosts, now can you? There are stories of things happening. And then there was the one about this boy and girl out parking in spite of the fact that they knew there was this escaped convict with a false hand that had a built in knife. And they heard this noise rap-tap-tapping on the side and top of the car, and they got real scared, and took off real fast. And when they finally got away, there was this false hand with a built in knife hanging from the door handle. You see, it is important to pay attention.

By this time, I wasn't exactly scared, but I didn't want any fooling around. I wanted to pay attention. There was some comfort in knowing we had our dog with us. It was of mixed parentage, sort of your generic dog, not good for much, but we had it along with us. I kept glancing at that dog to make sure it wasn't sensing anything out of the ordinary, because dogs can sense things that humans can't. They can tell when somebody had died way far away, or when spirits come around. So far that dog was just laying by the fire, legs sticking out, soaking up the heat, breathing easy, and eyes at half-staff.

Then that dog raised up its head and looked. I noticed that right away. The other guys didn't. I saw that dog get up and walk stiff-legged a couple steps out to the boundary of the light. It growled a bit. "What you reckon that dog is looking at?" I asked. Nobody seemed to know. By that time, we were all looking and listening. That dog got to woofing a bit. Its hair started to stand up. "Better hold that dog back," Jared said. "I do believe there is something out there."

I tried to hold it back. That dog didn't like hands put on it very much at that point of its life. It resisted. I just grabbed it by the collar and hoped for the best, but the best didn't come. It just got worse. We heard a thrashing in the woods, coming our way. "Something's coming," I informed the boys. "I don't know what it is." Neither did that dog. It was barking in a steady fashion now, with its lips curled back and its teeth shining in the firelight. This is not a good sign.

The rest of the boys sort of hung back by the fire, shuffling around, scratching and spitting, trying to be brave. This whole thing was bothering me quite a bit. I tried to tell the boys we ought to go on out there to figure this thing out, but they would just as soon stay by the fire. That dog sure wanted to go. "I am going to let this dog go," I announced. "Maybe it will chase whatever it is away." "Don't you do that," Jared commanded. "That might not be a safe thing to do. Whatever it is might hurt that dog." I tried to wait, but it is hard to be patient when you are liked to be scared to death.

Whatever it was kept on coming closer and closer. That dog just went hysterical. It left off regular style barking. It wasn't howling. It wasn't whimpering. It was a high-pitch soprano scream, going i-i-i-i with barely a pause for breath. It was slobbering so bad that it liked to nearly drowned itself when it did take an occasional breath. Now if your dog is scared like that, that is a sure sign.

I said to my brother, "Here, you hold this dog. I am going to get me a stick." Jared, he said, "You hadn't ought to do that." "But I got to do something," I replied. It was getting time for action. I was good and tired of being scared.

Then whatever it was ran up the side of a tree one side and down just as fast on the other side. "Holy cow," Jimmy moaned. "Did-ya see THAT? They's something out there." Up and down, up and down. All the boys were shocked into silence.

Because Jared said so, I had dropped the stick. By that time I had just had it. I picked up a big old rock, and said, "I'm moving out." "Don't you do that," Jared yelled. "You might make it mad." "I'm-a goin' out," I said with the conviction that sheer terror brings. "I'm-a gonna hurt that thing. I'm-a gonna run it off."

Jared was yelling, "Stop! Stop!" The rest of the guys didn't say nothing. They just hung back next to the fire with the whites of their eyes gleaming. If it was a spirit, a rock wouldn't hurt it. And if it wasn't, then, well, I guess we would just find out. I drew back, and Jared got all wild. "Stop it! Stop it!" he screamed. "I'm-a going," I muttered. "Naw! Naw! Stop it! It's my old man!"

Jared's old man stepped out from behind that tree just a-grinning. Jared, he took to laughing and jeering all by himself. "He sure scared you boys! I told him to come on up here and scare you boys. He sure scared you real bad. I knew it was him all along." Here he had snuck up on us, hid behind a tree, and ran his cap up and down the side of the tree just for fun. In among the shadows and darkness, augmented by vivid imaginations, it was easy mistake that hat for a creature from your nightmares.

Everybody except me went hee-hee-hee. "You sure was skeered, Kenny," they said. Yes I was, and that is a fact. Another fact is this: so were they, but I was the only one willing to do something about it.

The Principle of the Thing

Going to school when you are a kid is a good thing, I suppose, because you learn about spelling. Spelling can be sort of confusing because there are words that sound alike but have different spellings. And some words don't spell at all like they sound. The useless part is when they make you spell words that you will never use, and make you practice by using them in sentences. I mean to tell you what. That doesn't make any sense at all, and some of those sentences were absurd. It is a problem to use words when you don't know what they mean and have to copy them out of the spelling book to get the letters arranged right.

They taught us about the difference between aisle and isle. One of the differences is an extra letter - an "a" at the start of one of those words. I knew about aisle, and that every church had an aisle in it. The purpose of the aisle was for when you got saved. You had to walk down the aisle to the front to get saved. That is how it was done. The aisle was in the middle, not along the side. And if a church was big enough to have two center aisles, they likely didn't believe in getting saved publicly because there is only one way to Jesus, and that is down the center aisle in a very visible manner. None of this slinking down the sidelines, no sir.

So I knew all about aisle. Isle without an "a" was a useless word, because what that meant was island. We didn't have no isles in Knoxville. Isles were for poems and foreign places. There wasn't any purpose in isle; it was a needless word. But they had it in the spelling book just to confuse things. Not only did I have to learn about the word and how to spell it, I had to use it in a sentence. Well sir, I learned about that word. I wanted to use it creatively. "I went to an isle" seemed to be a rather meaningless sentence, so I cast about for a sentence that would have just a little bit more punch. So, being as we believed in sending out missionaries and being witness and all, I figured that I could discharge my Christian duty right there in Lonsdale Elementary School, just like I was taught to. I figured that an isle was a way faraway place and people there didn't have the gospel because it was so remote, and certainly they needed the blessings of salvation. So I wrote, "The preacher was in the isle."

Wrong. It got marked wrong. Now I knew better than that. I thought that was a double duty use of the word, being as aisle and isle sounded alike. Everybody that went to a Bible-believing church knew about a preacher being in the aisle, especially when they got earnest about salvation. But who said they couldn't save people in far-away places also? That is what I had in mind, and to this day I know in my heart that I was right when I wrote, "The preacher was in the isle."

It was just so confusing.

Now some of the tricks we learned about spelling were helpful. Separate, for example. That was what we were supposed to be. Separate from the world. That was an important word to get right. Only worldly people would spell it "seperate." I learned to look for a rat in separate to make sure you spelled it right. I bet every Mennonite child raised in the 1950's got that word right. Us Mennonites knew all about that word. I was proud to get that right and felt lofty when others didn't know better and spelled it with an "e" rather than an "a." When you grow up Mennonite in Knoxville, you take your pleasures wherever you can.

Now we get to the really important stuff - principle and principal. The principal was your pal, they said, and that is how you could tell the difference. Well, that helped with spelling principal and knowing what the word meant, and with knowing how to spell the other word, but not with knowing what principle meant. That was a hard word to understand. The only sentence I could make out of that was, "There is the principle of the thing."

You see, I heard that a lot, but no matter how often I heard it, I still didn't get it. I understood rules, but I didn't get principles. I gathered that principles were serious stuff, and that it was important to be sound and to have principles, but for the life of me I had no conception of what either of those words meant. And it was risky business to ask about either one of them, because faces would get red, cheeks and neck waddles would quiver when soundness and principles were discussed. The sound and fury about principles discouraged inquiry into these matters.

So I had to work on understanding principles all on my own and came up with a sort of a working understanding of them. Number one, it was important to have them, even if you didn't know what they were, and it was important to hold on to them even unto death. It was good to die for your principles. It was good to stand up like Daniel for your principles. I thought it would be even better if you knew what the principle of the thing actually was, but I guess that was less important that standing on it, somehow.

I kept working on this thing, watching and waiting for illumination. I gathered that principles were mostly unpleasant things to have to have, and jammed you up life, sort of like constipation. There seemed to be some sort of similarity between principles and constipation, near as I could figure out by observation and personal experience. Both caused feelings of confinement, but one was perpetual misery and the other was more short term.

Principles seemed to have to do with The Slippery Slope and with Ramifications. "Where will it all end? Once you give in an inch, it you might as well as give it all up." Ramifications were sort of like when you ended up where you didn't want to because of The Slippery Slope, but you didn't know it until you got there, but others could have told you so if you would of listened.

That Slippery Slope business was dangerous because of The Ramifications. You could never tell where it would all end, and having principles meant you weren't supposed to start anything unless the end was sound and sensible according to Scripture. That limited initiative in certain areas and created a considerable amount of internal anxiety, especially when those adolescent hormones got activated.

Principles and hormones don't work too well together. There was a rule regarding girls that ran something like this: touch not, taste not, handle not. And then another one was a prohibition against trifling with affections. I think the Slippery Slope principle was behind it all, but I wasn't for sure. It bothered me that all the rules and principles seemed to have a "no" rather than a "go" connected with them. That was so agonizing.

And how I agonized, very severely, when we went for a hike in the Smokey Mountains and the youth group from over in Hickory, North Carolina joined us. There was this girl over there in Hickory that made me want to forget all about rules, except for that muffled but constant drumming of principle holding me back. That was so inconvenient. When I say holding me back, that is exactly what I mean. I just could not move forward.

Me and some of the boys were walking an appropriate distance behind the group of girls. I had to worship her from afar, with downcast eyes. I saw how she wore her sneakers without socks and was just amazed. I marveled at the smooth curves of the calf muscles, admired the gentle fold of the back of the knee, and got hypnotized by the back and forth swishing of the hem on her khaki skirt. I dared not look higher for fear of being struck blind by God's wrath.

I thought, well, reckon if I could just move up a little and walk along side of her for a bit. Would that be a possibility? I tried to move forward, and actually did a step or two. I was sort of encouraged because she was at the end of the girls' pack, and even though I wasn't sure, I kindly imagined that she was lagging back a wee tiny little bit. But I didn't want to marry her just yet, because I didn't really know her. But that is what would happen if I moved too far forward. Or I would have to break up with her I didn't know how to do that. Or what if she actually WANTED me to walk with her? What if she

146

wanted to hold my hand? Where would this end? Then she would tempt me beyond that which I was able to withstand. I just didn't know what to do. It was horrible. The Ramifications terrified me.

So there I was, a sweaty and quivering mass of insufficiency, caught between earthly desires and principles. I was in soul agony, fueled by hormones and mandates. Couldn't move forward three more steps, couldn't back up three steps. No resolution, no comfort, no satisfaction.

Later on while we were doing dishes, I overheard her commenting about me being a woman-hater. Now that wasn't true at all, but unlike the preacher being in the isle without an "a", I couldn't and didn't say a word about it until this very moment because of the principle of the thing, whatever that means.

D'Alley

You never rightly know what influences sneak up unawares when you grow up Mennonite in Knoxville. The world was there, which was no big surprise, and we thought we did mostly well in keeping it in its rightful place, which was at arm's length. For example, we didn't hold pride and pretension in very high esteem. Addresses with apostrophes and hyphenated last names? Who ever heard of such stuff? It wasn't needful. It smacked loudly of pride. These things were worldly; they were Not To Be.

Mind you, this was back in the days when a Mennonite was a Mennonite and the world was the world. Things were much simpler that way, especially if you didn't have to deal with both of them at the same time.

I had heard of Arlington. That was where the Tomb of the Unknown Soldier was located and where the honor guards marched. My father was very respectful of Arlington. And I had heard of Darlington, which was very suspicious right on the face of it, because it sounded like darling. Later on I found out it was actually spelled with an apostrophe, d'Arlington, because of the French. The French believed in kissing, drinking wine, and being deceitful in spelling. It was good to have nothing to do with things French because of the influences. Even French dressing was a bit risqué - that was pushing the limits because white salad dressing out of a quart jar was good enough.

This business of being disdainful of pretentious ways made it hard to understand where this little girl lived. The adults were trying to invite her to come to Bible School, there at the Knoxville Mennonite Mission. She was hanging around, looking like Bible School would be good for what ailed her. "Where do you live?" they asked her. "Over on D'Alley," she replied. That was a bit rich for our blood. D'Alley. Huh. And besides, where was it at? Never heard of that street in Knoxville, unless it was in some sophisticated part of town. They asked her again. "Where?" "Just right over there," she pointed with her nose, with her mouth drooping open. "Right over yonder on d'alley."

Aha! Got it! She didn't have a street address, like 909 University Avenue or 1018 Connecticut Avenue. No, she lived right over there on the alley.

That sort of stopped the conversation cold. Somehow it didn't seem right to invite someone to our Bible School if they didn't have a proper address. D'Alley wasn't precise enough. And it wasn't Biblical, either. You could go to the highways and byways and compel them to come in, but there was no mention of alleys. Actually we didn't do real good with compelling people, but we didn't even try real hard when it came to alleys.

For starters, those old boys across the alley there at Lonsdale. We didn't invite them to Bible School. We threw rocks at them and bombarded their shed from the roof of our shed with bricks. We would never think of doing that on a street or avenue. In the alleyways of our Knoxville existence, life took on a different texture.

Poor old Abner of dark skin found out about that time after time. He lived across the street, just down from Flagpole Hill, there at the Knoxville Mennonite Mission. Old Willy, the preacher's boy would have encounters with Abner on the roof of the shed, which faced d'alley. Abner came out second best on these adventures. Circumstances being as they were, it was not in Abner's best interests to fight back. He would moan and groan most piteously. He would cry, with big rolling tears. "Oh, Weelie, please, doan' hit me no mo'." Life got just too miserable for Abner, especially as things were so one-sided. "I migh' as will roll off and keel myself," Abner choked out, as he lay on the flat roof of the shed, prostrate with grief and persecution.

I was watching all of this from the safety of ground level and at an adequate distance from that angel of death Willy. Abner was dealing with alley life up close and personal, closer to the edge than he realized. Suiting action with word, he rolled over, and his leg dropped over the edge of the roof.

Abner screamed, "Huh-WAAAHHHHH!" He teetered and flailed on the balance between wallops from Willy and bouncing off the ground. It was clear that he had a change of mind about rolling off the roof of the shed. The dramatic flair of his scream was highly entertaining, and lent him a brief stay of torture for the rest of that day.

Nowadays, I am quite comfortable with French dressing. I have been known to sip now and again on a wee tiny glass of wine. A few people unrelated to me got kissed. Whether it was French-style or not is none of your business. Irregular spellings, apostrophes and hyphenated names don't bother me much at all unless it is something stupid like Swartzentruber-Stoltzfus. That stuff isn't real serious, heavy duty worldly encroachment.

No sir. What really bothers me about then and now is alley living.

Whisper A Prayer

Mind you, we believed in praying, back when I grew up Mennonite in Knoxville, because you were supposed to. That was something you did out loud before each and every meal, at night time, at prayer meeting, at church, and before you went on trips. You were supposed to pray basically all the time, because of that song:

> "Whisper a prayer in the morning,
> Whisper a prayer at noo-oo-oon,
> Whisper a prayer in the evening,
> To keep your heart in tune."

We sang that song a lot at church, and I felt guilty every time because without fail I forgot to whisper a prayer morning, noon, and evening.

Another song, "E'er You Left Your Room This Morning, Did You Think to Pray," went on to promise:

> "Oh, how praying rests the weary,
> Prayer will change the night to day.
> So when life seems dark and dreary,
> Don't forget to pray."

I guess that is why my life seemed so dark and dreary, because Satan made me to forget to pray.

Satan was sneaky about that business of causing you to forget things like praying. Another thing. If you had sin in your life, God couldn't hear your prayers, unless it was the Sinner's Prayer. That was supposed to be a heavy duty, serious prayer that bulldozed the way through and would make God pay attention. I guess you could say I didn't grasp the prayer concept very well.

Even though I didn't figure it out well, I got to understand the rules pretty good. You weren't supposed to pray like the Catholics because their prayers didn't count. Those prayers did not come from the heart. They were written by somebody else and had to be said just the right way, so you knew they were insincere. Plus, those prayers didn't go straight to God anyhow. They had to be delivered by a saintly postmaster and reviewed by Mary the Mother of God first to see if it was proper for God to hear. Huh. We believed in one-stop praying to Dear Jesus in Heaven, a straight through prayer with no detour or filtering.

So that was one kind of prayer that didn't count. Another kind was like what your generic Bab-dis' and Holy Rollers did, where they would all pray at the same time. And they would say "Lord" after every three words, which was clearly vain repetition. Bible said so. It was a noisy, confusing time, and how was God supposed to hear all that stuff at the same time. That was praying like the heathen. Those prayers weren't done decently and in good order. You couldn't count on a regular ending. Things would sort of fade away, until there would be one voice hanging in until they realized they were praying all alone, and then the end would be announced with a hasty "Heeeeey-man!"

No, you were supposed to be dignified when you prayed, and be sincere about it for it to have any chance to being heard. And it was best to be a bit tentative about things, and not ask for too much or expect too much. It was okay to ask, as long as you added the small print, the disclaimer of "if it be according unto Thy will." That would keep you from getting your hopes up too high.

Instead of praying loudly and aggressively, we were supposed to whisper a prayer, very reverently. It was more comforting that way. And it worked better if you could get someone else to pray for you, unless it was some Catholic saint you called on. Our preacher, Brother Ezra, understood praying for others very well, because at prayer meeting he had this method. He would ask for prayer requests, and you could list them out loud for everyone to hear. And then he would say, "While every head is bowed and every eye is closed, raise your hand if you have an unspoken request." There would be this holy

154

silence, while he would scan the audience and say, "Yesssss, I see that hand. Yesssss. And that one. Yesssss. God Bless You. And that one. Yesssss." I always wanted to peep to see who had unspoken requests, but I never dared. During other times you could sneak a look, but not while every head was bowed and every eye was closed. That was too sacred of a moment to tamper with.

It was comforting to have Brother Ezra pray for you. And even though I would never admit it, I was warmed to hear my parents say that they prayed "for you children ever since before the day you were born." I wanted to get comfort, and have it on tap for myself, but it didn't seem like my prayers made it through. I guess there was too much static on the line, or my accumulated sins provided too thick of a barrier and I couldn't figure out how to make a good-enough Sinner's Prayer. I didn't derive a whole lot of predictable comfort from my whispered prayers.

There is one prayer for sure that did not comfort me in the very least. It burned me to the core. It wasn't one I made up, either. It was one my brother did.

He wanted to be in our bedroom all alone there at 1018 Connecticut Avenue to work on his model airplane. I wasn't in favor of this at all, because I was being excluded. I wanted to watch and interfere if at all possible. He did not want company or interference. He wanted me to be far away, like far beyond the Northern Sea. Naturally, being I was who I was, I persisted, and a pushing contest ensued, me on one side of the door and he on the other. Words were exchanged. My glee increased.

But the fun stopped abruptly as I heard a soft voice coming from the other side of the door. It was not a whisper, but a still, small voice praying. It was my brother praying to Jesus, and he was praying for me. He prayed that Jesus would help me be a good boy. It was not an official prayer, written by some saint long time ago. It was not filled with vain repetition. It was quiet, sincere, and to the point. The kind of prayer that Jesus obviously heard and approved of. The kind of prayer that gets action.

Oh, I felt so bad. I was shamed into silenced and out of the house. I had to go sit out on the front porch to recover. "There you go again," I thought to myself. I just laminated another sinful action to the ceiling of my prayer closet so my own prayers couldn't make it through.

Strictly speaking, that prayer, even though it was an approved prayer, didn't get answered. I did not turn into a good boy. But at least my brother got what he needed, which was a brief respite from Ken-induced annoyance.

Well, sir. It was clear I was in deep water in the praying department. That is why I took to whispering a prayer now and again, hoping that one or two might slip through a crack or a knothole somewhere, because if you pray too hard, too loud, or with too big of expectations, they just bounce back on you.

Brother Ezra is dead and gone by now, but maybe over yonder in Glory Land he will remember my name and whisper a prayer on my behalf. Maybe in the dead of the night, while every eye is closed, I will raise my hand for him to see. I bet he will see it. I bet he will see my hand and say, "Yesssss, I see that hand. Bless you." That is comforting.

Yes, sir. Maybe those Catholics weren't too far off the mark to have a saint on the other side to help out a little bit. If their saints are anything like Brother Ezra, it won't hurt at all, and might even be useful to enlist their aid.

"Whisper a Prayer in the Morning," Public Domain
"Did You Think To Pray," Mary A. Kidder, Pub. 1897, Public Domain

Silver Bells

We didn't make a whole lot out of Christmas back when I was growing up Mennonite in Knoxville. Christmas trees and lots of decorations were worldly, while buying more than one gift per person offended the principle of frugality. Christmas parties? Everybody knew that was flirting with danger because, well, because things could happen at Christmas parties, what with mistletoe and all. It was best not to dwell on these things.

We did have some Christmas traditions in the House of Yoder, including pulling out the paper-cups-covered-with-aluminum-foil bells, the cardboard Nativity set, a string of small colored lights, a can of artificial snow and a stencil set. Since I was not to be trusted with the can of snow, I would carefully hold the stencil set while my Mother would spray in careful, short bursts, and presto, there on the window would be the words "Merry Christmas" and "Noel." If it was a good year, there would also be an artificial snow wreath with a candle and a few blasts of snow in the corner of the window panes. That was so special, and with careful management, one can would last at least three years.

We would have nuts set out, like pecans and Brazil nuts. Hard candy to suck on, and once in a great while, chocolate covered crème drops. Call me old fashioned, I don't care, but they don't make chocolate covered crème drops like they used to. Along around Thanksgiving time Mom took to baking date pinwheel cookies but wouldn't let us have any. She hid them all over the place, and if she caught us snooping, she would say,

> Mousie, oh mousie,
> go quickly away.
> These are not for you.
> They are for our Christmas Day.

That didn't keep us away for real. It just helped us get

sneakier. Found them, too, every year but one, when Mother hid them in the washing machine. My brother and I were so disgusted. Here we were, adult men, finding each other sneaking around, and both of us not finding those daggone cookies.

There in Knoxville, they had this great big huge Christmas tree on top of the parking garage across from Rich's Department store. It would get lit up during the Christmas season, with lots of fanfare. Up to 20,000 people would turn out for the event. Six high school choirs, one in each stairwell landing at either end of Rich's would sing in turn. The lights would be turned on for each choir when it was their time to sing. And then, the grand finale - a girl was selected to sing "O Holy Night," and at the critical time, all lights in the stairwells would come on, all six choirs would sing out, "FA-AA-AA-ALL on your knees..." and the Christmas tree lights came on. It was so grand.

It was no small task to keep all six choirs together. I imagine it was J. B. Lawson, over there in the parking lot, beating time with a flashlight, and Mr. Bentley, our choir director, looked back over his shoulder and tried to keep us all together.

Oh, man, we looked forward to Christmas. We put up with the Sunday School program at church as best we could. We knew the real meaning of Christmas already, and could recite flawlessly the first 20 verses of Luke 2: "And it came to pass in those days that there went out a decree from Caesar Augustus that all the world should be taxed." OK. Christmas was about Jesus' birthday and all that. Got it. Let's get on with the good stuff already.

My younger sister nearly spoiled one Christmas for me, and I haven't quite gotten over it yet. Our family recited the Christmas story and then opened our presents. Oh boy. A triple pack of Fruit of the Loom underwear, and just my size with a little extra room to grow in. We had to learn to be thankful for getting the things we really needed, versus getting what we wanted because wants fade away or change, but what you really need and should be thankful is clean underwear in case you are in an accident and have to go to the hospital. The first thing they do in the emergency room is to take your underwear off and check to see if they are clean. But anyhow.

After the predictable round of presents, Dad pulled out this white, oblong box. A train set! A Happy Time Electric Train, with a locomotive, coal car, closed cargo car, open cargo car, and a caboose. Four sections of straight and eight sections of curved, 3-rail track. We played very carefully with that train set, and then put it back in the box, just exactly right, so it would last a long time. My brother and I sat there, just gazing on the box, and then my little sister went and ruined it all. She took and propped her stinky, messy, tiny little old feet right on top of the box. She wasn't allowed to play with the train, much less touch the box, and there she goes tromping her feet all over the box. That level of disrespect, disregard, and distain was just too much to bear. What would she do next? Paint the engine pink? Put baby dolls in the cargo car? Girls just don't understand about trains, much less trains at Christmas. I wish to this very day she wouldn't of done that.

As bitter-sweet as that year was, better times were in store. One year we got invited to Saint Mary's Hospital School of Nursing Christmas Party, and we actually went. I knew it would be special, because there was a big Christmas tree, piled with tons of presents wrapped with a lavish hand. Sister Mary Whatever directed me away from the punch bowl I was headed to, and said to my father with a meaningful nod, "That punch there is for the children." I didn't understand at the time what that was about, but afterwards and with mature reflection, I think Sister wanted us to avoid looking through a glass darkly, as it were.

Then the student nurses paraded out for a program. They sang so sweetly, and I fell in love with them individually and corporately. They sang in three-part harmony, but not like Mennonite women sang. It was

159

light, crisp, and absolutely divine. It was better than the Mennonite Hour ladies' chorus. I sat there, entranced and enthralled as those southern belles sang about silver bells:

"Silver bells, (silver bells),
Silver bells, (silver bells),
It's Christmas time in the city (oo-oo-oo-ah)
Hear them ring (hear them ring),
Ding-a-ling (ding-a-ling),
Soon it will be Christmas Day."

It was Christmas time, I was plump with punch, surrounded by beautiful music and beautiful student nurses, and filled with amorous feelings. It don't get any better than that.

Somewhere I know there is a perfect silver bell that sends out a perfect sound to evoke a perfect Christmas. It does not exist in a material sense at all, but more as an idea. All other bells, silver or otherwise, including paper cups covered with aluminum foil, are just a reflection of the perfect ideal. But whenever I see a silver bell, hear a silver bell go ding-a-ling, or sing about a silver bell, my mind goes back, way back, when times were simpler and we got close to the ideal Christmas, right there in Knoxville.

"Silver Bells," Jay Livingston and Ray Evans, released 1950

160

Sensitive Points

If you want my opinion, here it is. I happen to think advice or directives work best if the one in charge knows what he or she is talking about. Or at least can make you believe that is the case. I have to admit that was a sensitive point with me, back when I was growing up Mennonite in Knoxville.

It seemed like there was a limitless supply of opportunity to get into prickly situations, even without having to work very hard at it. I mean, it is one thing to knowingly push into a blackberry bramble to get the nicest blackberries. You knew what the prize was, you could clearly envision blackberry cobbler, and then you could figure out how many thorns and chiggers you wanted to risk. That was a rather easy equation to work out. I mean, those thorns could scratch the dickens out of you, and those nasty little chiggers were horrible. But it was worth it, especially when you had a choice in the matter.

Blackberries - now that is one thing. I could handle that. Other points of sensitivity just escaped me. It was like getting ambushed without any satisfaction coming out of it. Sensitivities abounded in rich supply, and I just couldn't figure it out. There would be these looks, full of meaning, but I was just too little or too dense to figure out what the meaning was.

Take for example. We had a furnace in the floor there at the Knoxville Mennonite Mission, with a grate you could stand on. It was located in the center aisle, towards the front. That was nice, especially on a cold Sunday evening. The heat would rise up so nice and toasty. About the only warm spot in the whole establishment, if you want to get right down to it. It made sense to me to stand there before or after church. The men could stand there and warm up. But there must have been a point of sensitivity, because I heard the men

161

complaining about how the girls would stand there. "This is <u>Not Good</u>," I heard proclaimed, in serious tones that tolerated no dissention. Not good. I wondered about that. I listened for knowledge, because you need to know what is not good, and then decide how much of it you wanted to try out. I think it was <u>Not Good</u> on account of the disturbing fact that the rising heat would make the girl's dresses flair out just a wee tiny bit. I don't know for sure. Maybe there were more mature considerations. Maybe that warm air would go all the way up to you know where. That HAD to be not good. Some things are best left unwarmed. You know what I mean.

My mom was good at discovering sensitive points and then leaving me to figure this thing out. I just knew I had transgressed, but didn't know how I had managed to do it yet again. Just being overwhelmed with guilt for doing something that was, nod, nod, meaningful gaze, *too bad,* removed any thought about the benefits of trying it again. All thorns and no cobbler, that is what that was like. How was I to know if it was *too bad* if I didn't even know what I had done in the first place? Is it too much to ask for clarity in these issues?

One of the sensitive points had to do with that Bell and Howell reel-to-reel tape recorder we had. It could handle 7 inch tape reels, and did we ever use that machine. I learned to really appreciate gospel music and the Mennonite Hour singers from that tape player. Hours and hours of listening, nurturance, and refreshment. Even when I couldn't understand the words I could sense the fervor and richness of my heritage. Decades later I still hear those songs, as Brother Ezra would say, in my mind's eye.

And, we had a lot of pleasure in making our own recordings. There was this microphone with a 1/4 inch plug to stick in the jack in the front of the machine. Turn the knob to "record," twist the handle to "play/record," and that is all it took. Except. Yeah, you got it. That microphone cord had a sensitive point. I guess I wasn't very careful, and I dinged the plug on the floor.

That turned into a teaching moment. I learned about the word sensitive for the first time. My mother yelped, grabbed my neck by one hand and the microphone cord by the other. "That is sensitive," she said, with great intensity. "Careful. That point is *sensitive*." I must have looked hard to impress about these things, because the lesson was drilled home. "Look! Right there! See! That is *sensitive*," she continued, pointing to the end of the jack.

Well, I didn't know sensitive, and I didn't know what was sensitive about a pointy piece of metal. You didn't talk into that end, I didn't think, so I couldn't figure out what was so special about it except that you plugged it in, and there was sort of a notch when you pushed it in all the way. That must have been the sensitive point.

It took me years to get comfortable with a 1/4 inch jack. Even now I wince when a patch cord is dropped. Which doesn't make any sense at all except that is I how I first learned about sensitive.

There really isn't anything wrong about sensitivity, I guess, as long as you are talking about the right end of the cord. And if it comes to a decision between eating blackberry cobbler or banging a microphone jack on the floor, well, there is no contest.

Hot Spots

I guess you can say that I got into a hot spot or two in the course of my life. There were some opportunities to find hot spots while I was growing up Mennonite in Knoxville and I seemed to find them from time to time, and I know I am responsible for going there when I shouldn't have. On the other hand, hot spots would find me once in a while. I don't know why it worked out that way, but that is the way it went. Still had to deal with the consequences.

There was this time that I was walking home from school, all by myself. It seemed like I did a lot of walking home all by myself. Sometimes, instead of walking along Connecticut Avenue like I was supposed to, I would sneak up the alley for a block or two and come to our house from the alley side. That was a bit more adventurous, because you could never tell what you might encounter in the alley. Going up the front side of the houses, along the avenue route, felt safer. The alley way, looking into the back yards, was a lot more unpredictable. There is a decided difference between the front and back views of life there in Lonsdale. Most often I went home the proper way, walking up on the left hand sidewalk of Connecticut Avenue. It is good to know which side of the street you better stay on. And I was on the right side, near as I could tell.

I guess I wasn't paying close attention to my surroundings like I should have been. I was lulled into a false sense of security because it was a fine autumn afternoon, and the trees were luminescent in the afternoon sun with their brightly colored leaves. The sidewalk was covered with autumn leaves. That is what I was paying attention to - those leaves. They were so pretty and colorful. I thought they were sort of like big flowers and I wanted to collect some and take them home to my mother. Maybe she would be pleased with this. But I got to tell you something. Be aware of pretty things, because that will take your eyes of the dangers that surround you.

I had just found this remarkable leaf with pure white blotches in it. That leaf was as big as my head, and I had room enough in my left hand to hold on to it. I was thinking about this special leaf when a hot spot fell upon me. "Hey, boy!" only it sounded more like "Hey bo-ah!" "Hey, boy! Whatcha doing with those leaves? You better leave them alone. I'm-a coming to get you on account of you stealing my leaves. I'm-a gonna keel you."

I was just a first grader, much too young to die, and normally I couldn't run very fast. Buddy, I tell you what. I flung those leaves and lit out for home like the devil and all his angels were after me, which as far as I knew was exactly the case. It looked like a sixth grader, but I knew the devil could take many forms. I ran so fast I couldn't stop at Johnson Street - just went across it, my little legs going up and down like valve stems. Crossing Johnson Street at full tilt without stopping to look carries some measure of risk. You can get killed that way. There wasn't much time to consider things, because behind me was certain death but ahead of me was just the possibility of death. Moments like that, you just do the best you can and make a snap decision. Across I went. I was all out of wind but fear kept me going. Up past the Richard's' house, past the Cantrell's house, across our lawn. I was running much too fast to open the screen door, but I knew there were limits placed on running through them. No sir. No point in going through closed doors. It is better to die on Johnson Street than to run through the screen door, or come to think of it, to even slam that door. I was gasping my last breaths, my rubbery legs got me to the slanty cellar door, you know, the one you weren't supposed to play on, but this seemed to be a special circumstance. I collapsed on that slanty door, eyes closed in agony, wheezing and heaving, toes pointed heavenward, hoping the end would be a bit less painful. I thought I might be safe from my tormenter, but there was that heart attack about to happen. I was near death. They would find me stretched out on that door with a look of mortal agony on my face, and it would be awful. I practiced what that last grimace would look like until I thought I had it right. I kept waiting for someone to come by so I could tell them I was having a heart attack, but nobody seemed to notice anything. This was not good. Not good at all. But I survived. Never did find the leaves I flung away in my haste, because it took me a couple months to gain the courage to go looking.

Actually, there may be a redeeming feature about hot spots. Maybe they help build character. How would I know about that for sure? If that is the case, my character ought to be in better shape than its current condition. Seems like I have wasted the benefit of hot spots.

Sometimes you get into hot spots because of being led astray. The temptation is just too great, like the time when nobody was looking and the seven-minute icing on the cake meant for company was just too enticing. Surely a wee tiny little finger swipe wouldn't be noticed. Wrong. Mother noticed. Mothers always notice. "What happened here? Who did this to my cake?" she asked. Oh boy. Heat was coming, and that was a fact that even I could catch on to. My little mind raced furiously. The line-up of potential culprits was remarkably limited. Attention was being focused upon me in a way that I did not like. Maybe I could get out of this without exactly lying, but diverting attention to another possibility. Yes! That is a chance I could take! Full of resolute intention, I looked at the tread mark in the icing, which by now looked like an 18-wheeler had plowed through it, arranged my face into an expression of pure shock, and gasped, very convincingly, about who in the world would consider such a thing. Surely not I.

Didn't work. Mother looked at me with a gaze of full reproof. "Now my nice cake for company is all messed up," she stated. "Now what am I going to do?" I felt awful, but the icing did taste good. And once again my character failed to benefit from the experience. And

167

as far as I can tell, none of these hot spots had a discernable positive impact on my character. Maybe I need some more practice. Somehow I doubt if it would help very much.

Ken Takes A Bath

There is a picture somewhere of me and my brother in a galvanized wash tub, way back when, long before either of us had reached the age of accountability. I figured this out with a fair degree of certainty because of two observations: We are just little kids, and we are both smiling. That is what innocence does to you - you think nothing is wrong about playing around in the water and smiling while you take a bath. After the age of accountability sets in, there isn't much to smile about, especially when it comes to naked bodies and water.

Before long, we learned that taking a bath was serious business. It was such serious business that one engaged in bath-taking only on Saturday night, so as to be clean for Sunday. Being clean for Sunday was important. That is why we needed to take a bath. There may have been symbolism involved here, because it was not proper to have any sort of uncleanness in the church come Sunday morning. Maybe that is why I sort of felt like an imposter in church, because the Bible said that God looks on the inside and can see that the cup is dirty when the hypocrites just tried to get by with washing the outside and pretending the inside was clean. It did make me wonder about the effectiveness of Saturday night baths. It just got the skin clean. Didn't seem to help out the inner part. Even I knew that.

The rest of the week we made do in the getting clean arena by washing our feet in the evenings. There was this 10-quart galvanized bucket and you would put water in it, get a bar of soap and a scrub brush, go sit down on the steps and get to work. If absolutely necessary, and under duress, one could wash up as far as half way to the knees.

Washing feet, hands, and faces - that was what happened between Saturday nights in the tub. And tub time was not for luxury - you got in the bath tub and got out, and saved the water for the next person in line. It didn't do to waste water, even though it was dirty and grey with soap. No tub toys, no soaking in hot water, no reading a book. We never once heard of a spa or a Jacuzzi or a hot tub. There was not one single solitary reason in the universe for lounging in a tub of hot water. That would not have been good stewardship to have more than four inches of lukewarm water. No sir. In, scrub, and out, with no dilly-dallying.

And to have silly stuff like bubble bath beads, well, we sort of had an inkling that such stuff existed, but not in the house of Yoder. Soap suds were for the wash machine, not the bath tub. Suds in a bath tub was a wasteful concept. Wasteful of money, wasteful of good hot water, wasteful of time.

Imagine, then, my surprise one time when I went to stay in my younger sister's house for a week and to care for Dad while they went away. I was given instructions to make myself at home. I shouldn't of listened to her at all. Wasn't my fault I nearly died.

You see, she has this master bathroom off of the master bed room. I walked in the bathroom, and great day in the morning, that bath tub was big as the Atlantic Ocean and held nearly a thousand gallons. Nozzles and jets all over the place, and the spigot off to the side, and not at the end where God intended it to be. Dials and buttons and everything. A purple mat thing somewhere, but you needed a telescope to make it out clearly. And some sort of other thing, also purple, that had branchy tentacles sticking out all around. That made me just a bit anxious, because I wondered what it was for, but couldn't think of any wholesome ideas. It was not the kind of bath tub I was used to. It was much too large for one person, and thinking about this made me nervous because of certain implications, such as, just how many people were supposed to be in there at the same time? My goodness, how things have changed. Our tub back in Knoxville barely held one person, and that is the way it is supposed to be, yesterday, today, and forever. I was soon to learn that the concepts of drift and a slippery slope were more than just a theological concern.

I figured, well, maybe I ought to try out a new experience since nobody was looking. I started running water in that tub, left it run for two three hours while I made supper and did the dishes and found a book to read. Came back in and it was nearly halfway full so I came to the conclusion that it was time to embark on an unknown journey that on the surface promised luxury.

Before I did that I noticed an extra detail. There were a couple of bottles on the far end of the tub. One was labeled French Lilac Bubbling Bath Oil and the other was Moisturizing Bath Beads. By this time I had lived long, hard years, with creature comforts few and far between. I was tempted. After a season of temptation, lasting around five seconds, I cut loose with the bath oil and dumped in a cup or so of the bath beads, and turned on the button that caused the high pressure water nozzles to squirt.

Now there was a problem I encountered soon, because as I held my book high and lowered myself into the tub, I couldn't see the bottom of the tub, being as there was already a thin layer of foam on the surface of the water and I wondered where that purple thingy with the fingers sticking out was. I didn't want any surprises. After I hit bottom safely, I leaned back and relaxed and read my book, hoping that no purple menace would sneak upon me in a way I did not like or approve of.

I noticed that there was a nice layer of suds, sort of like Cool Whip, and I thought, cool! and went on reading. After a while, I thought, well, how about just laying back all the way for the full effect and read your book in true luxury.

What happened next was totally uncalled for and nearly terminal. I did not know how slick the bottom of that tub was. And I did not exactly realize how thick that layer of suds was. I mean to tell you what. The intention of a gradual slip into the deep end of the tub resulted in slide, faster than down a sliding board while sitting on a piece of wax paper. My rear end headed in the direction of Europe at the speed of light, my right leg shot up in the direction of the North Star, one elbow caught the edge of the tub. I tried to keep my book dry, so my left hand was not too much use. All I had to work with was the little finger of my left hand, and that digit is not noted for its strength or durability. But it tried to slow things down by digging a groove on the top edge of that tub. The big toe on my left foot saved the day. It shot straight up the nozzle of the spigot, and sort of lodged side-wise and kept me from going any further.

They say at moments like this your life passes before your eyes. I don't know about that. I can only testify to what I experienced. First of all, there was this horrible burning sensation in my sinus cavities that left me know I was in deep trouble. Then I began to worry about that purple thing, with those finger-like extensions, being as I was all spraddled out and in sort of a vulnerable position, what with one toe up a spigot and the other foot making aimless waving motions high in the sky. I looked up, and it seemed like there were mountains of suds above my head, around three feet high. I knew you could die from water shooting up your nose real fast, but that danger was not an issue due to my jammed toe, although it was hurting a bit. I tried and tried to scoot my rear end back towards the United States but there was no grip. I worried about smothering under mounds of suds, because the nozzles were going full tilt, and the mounds were piling up by the minute. I guess I put a bit too much of the bubble stuff in, what with the action of the water pumps and all.

I truly don't know how I got untwisted and upright again. It must have been a miracle because I did eventually reverse course. Maybe the concern about that purple thing provided additional motivation. I am happy to be alive and unscathed. I pondered on what lesson I should learn from this episode that God sent my way, and honestly, I didn't come up with one. I will have to ponder on this a bit more. It may relate to a thought that growing up Mennonite in Knoxville wasn't so awful compared with certain modern so called conveniences that have more than a small element of mortal danger and are morally suspect.

I Use-ta Think

It was sort of automatic, you know. Those explanations for what was happening just came without a whole lot of aforethought. This situation is not unique to growing up Mennonite in Knoxville, but I didn't know that for a very long time. We had lots of explanations for basically anything that happened or could happen.

Take f'rinstance. If you had a bad time in school, like as if the teacher yelled at the whole class, and you mentioned it at home, there was this sure-fire response. "What did you do to cause this?" Never no allowance for the teacher having a bad hair day. Always my fault, never the teacher's fault. After a while, you learn about this, and think the same way. If anyone anywhere at any time gets upset, the explanation is that I caused that to happen. It is the only logical explanation. Kinda powerful on several levels if you set down and think about it.

There was this cosmic balance to things. Someone up there was watching and keeping account of things, and in the fullness of time there would payday. Never knew when, but it was coming, and it would be an awful surprise. So if there was an offense against the divine order of things, there had to be retribution, either immediately or sometime in the future. And to clear up any misunderstanding in this regard, it was best to clarify just what that retribution would be. It is helpful to know if you buy candy of a Sunday, it will turn sour in your stomach and make you throw up. If you play softball on the Sabbath, you will fall down and hurt yourself, or the ball will hit you in the eye. In some ways, it must have been the Sabbath every time I tried to play softball, because I was always having bad luck in that department. Ball hitting me in the eye and breaking my glasses. Trying to catch the ball in my mitt, only to have the ball land on my thumb and very nearly breaking it. With sober reflection, one could recognize there was some sort of misfeasance, malfeasance or nonfeasance that was at the root of this misfortune. Things don't just happen, you know. Things have a reason - they happen to get the divine scales in balance. After a while, you learn to understand this automatically.

After a lot of practice in this endeavor, one can have secret knowledge about the real meaning of things. Others don't see what you see. They don't understand the trends that are involved. They just go on their way, being optimistic and happy as can be. This is a sad state of affairs, because they have been misled, and their minds are not open and their spirits are not sensitive to the real nature of things. Being happy is a sure sign of being frivolous, of avoiding causes and consequences, of ignoring certain truths. What other explanation could there be?

You probably won't believe it, but I used to get persecuted a lot when I was little. I could never figure out a good reason for this unless it had something to do with predestination. It seemed everyone everywhere could read a sign on my forehead, sort of like the mark of Cain, which indicated that I was fair game for all manner of indignities. I just knew for sure that everyone was against me. Not to be overly dramatic about it, but that was the actual reality of things. With the certainty of secretly imparted wisdom, I could confirm the truth of this perception very quickly and frequently.

I would sing with heartfelt fervor and totally without a sense of irony:

Nobody likes me, everybody hates me,
Guess I'll go eat worms.
Great big slimy ones, little tiny wiggly ones,
Oh how they do squirm.

I use-ta think that was true, except for the eating worms part. I dint think eating worms would help too much, but the picture of being so rejected that eating worms seemed like a good idea felt real authentic. Everybody in the whole wide world would sing that song

176

to me when I was down in the dumps, I guess in an effort to cheer me right up. Can't say as it helped too much.

Well. There was this one time where I came to a certain conclusion about things. Whatever happened was so grievous that the memory of the exact details is not readily available. The outcome is that I lit out of the house and ran down the hill to the barn and climbed up into the hay mow so as to be all alone just to prove how abandoned I felt. But, my stinking brother. My stinking brother found me just to make fun of me because, I guess, it seemed like a good idea at the time. He went hee-hee-hee, and I bawled out loud, much too loud for my size and age. His merriment increased in proportion to my theatrical display.

Buddy, I mean to tell you what. It was just too much. A long life time of experiences consisting of 13 years crystallized at that moment, a sequence of thoughts became solidified into a deep belief. I created a brand new credo, and gave voice to it, not to very sympathetic ears, I might add.

I wailed out, "I use-ta think I know, but now I *know* I know!" You have to get this right to carry the full meaning. The voice has to be filled up and dripping over with desperate tearfulness, and on the second 'know' there needs to be a hysterical note, a great emphasis, a crescendo, a tidal overflow of conviction. There has to be the right measure of melodrama to get the full effect.

Well, I wish I could report that I was deeply understood for once in my life. Do you think I was? Not on your life. My brother, he went from hee-hee-hee to HAW-HAW-HAW, and being the stinker he was, he ran straight back up to the house to report on this latest Kenny-amusement for the enjoyment of the whole family.

Waddn't fair.

Well, that was way back then and this is now, but the memory is still alive. And it causes me to ponder on thinking and knowing. Thinking is one thing, powerful as it is, especially when you don't have to work at it, when it just comes naturally. Knowing is something else.

Sometimes these two things get sort of mixed up. These days I spend more time thinking about thoughts and the more I do that, the less I know for sure. Maybe it is better that way.

We got to hear lots of Bible stories way back then when I was growing up Mennonite in Knoxville, and I loved every one of them. Well, most of them if I have to be honest about it. There were so many of them to hear about. There were so many lessons to learn from them. I didn't do real good in learning the lessons. I couldn't understand the details of some of them stories - like when someone lay with someone else. What did that mean, for Pete's sake? And furthermore, some stories seemed to be good enough without figuring out the lesson, which I seemed to forget anyhow. No matter how you shake it out, I liked those stories a whole lot, maybe because they helped me make up some stories of my own.

I liked the story of the prodigal son and how he wasted his life in riotous living. That part sounded interesting, except for the part where he would fain to eat the husks fed to the hogs. Things turned out just fine, on account of he came home again and got a hero's welcome. That goes to show. You are supposed to have things turn out good if you go bad on account of if you stay good like the other brother then things get bad so what's the point. Thing was I didn't have much opportunity to get off the tracks too far. I was too afraid of the long arm of the law and the sting of my dad's belt. Both had an incredible reach across time and space. But I still wanted to have a bit of riotous living, just a little taste without anybody knowing about it.

The Bible was very important in our home, along with The Martyr's Mirror, Pilgrims Progress, and Heart Throbs. It got used a lot for reading and memorizing. I remember lots of those words because they ring so true. "He was a man of sorrows and acquainted with grief." That was a good one. There were a couple that confused me, like "He has made us p'taters," or we were supposed to "teach and astonish one another." My dad use to quote "Ye know not what we know." It is right there in the

Gospel of St. John, chapter 4, verse 22. That verse I could understand. That was a no brainer.

There were some other words and concepts in the Bible that were sort of useful when it came to making a good prayer. My dad excelled in weaving good thoughts in his prayers, like "Set a watch on our lips and guard our thoughts." I figured that one might have application, because my lips and thoughts needed extra help beyond what I could offer on my own steam. You would think with such a sincere, heartfelt, poetic prayer, would get good results. I am sad to say there is more than ample evidence that my prayer has not yet been fully answered. Seems like I specialize in foolish words and thoughts.

My dad would often end his prayers with "...and keep us until Jesus comes." I liked that a lot. It was comforting to hear that. It seemed like a good idea to enlist the help of the Almighty in enduring until the end.

But, laying all seriousness aside, I have to tell you something. Those proverbs were troublesome, because many of them talked about fools and wise people. I had no difficulty recognizing which was my category. My dad would quote to me on more than one occasion, with deep sighs, intermittent shaking of the head, and downcast eyes: "A wise son maketh a glad father, but a foolish son is the heaviness of his mother." There seemed to be a message in there for me in a personal sort of way and I didn't have to study on it very hard to sort out the meaning. It was clear even for me to pick up on. Especially being as I heard it so much, and in so many contexts. That is a good way to memorize Scripture when you hear it a lot and then you ponder on it.

The verdict was in. I was foolish son. I was not a wise son based on the results mentioned in that verse. There wasn't much evidence of one part and a bit too much of the other. So there you have it.

I wanted to be wise, because of the responsibility that the Bible put on my shoulders. It was a heavy load to bear. I tried and tried to do better, but I just didn't get it. The harder I worked at it, it didn't matter at all. I just got more foolish in a sequential and cumulative fashion. There had to be a reason for this, even though I couldn't figure it out. Ever'buddy else around me had wisdom. I just knew they knowed I was foolish because, well, that is the way things came out.

I pondered and pondered on this thing. What was the secret of wisdom and how did you get it? How did you get to be so foolish? So much time and energy spent on those questions. Now, what I did not know at the time was this: When you ponder too much on certain things that don't have good answers, you might wind up being foolish rather than getting wiser.

Me and My Fingernail

You see, it was like this. Back before Christmas, my dear wife set up the Christmas tree. I should have known trouble was coming because we never had a Christmas tree back when I was growing up Mennonite in Knoxville. Setting up a Christmas tree was one of those things Not Done, so that we could be a witness and be separate from the world around us. We did have little tiny colored lights that would glisten like the Star of Bethlehem if you looked at them through a vial of cod liver oil pills.

Well, the lights this year didn't work. Half of them in the line worked, half didn't. So it was up to The Man of the House to fix this thing, never mind if he had nary an idea of what to fix or even how to fix it. Maybe it was the fuse. Or a short. I figured on this and looked at the picture on the box that indicated there was this fuse in the plug but not how to get to it near as I could tell.

So in true masculine fashion I took a knife and a screwdriver to the plug. And of course I paid for the overload of testosterone - I rammed my right index finger right up against the plug and lifted my finger nail. I did not see any Stars of Bethlehem or anything sweet like that at all. Don't ask me what I said or did because it's none of your business, but I will say it stung a little bit. Bled a bit, too. Kathy tried to be solicitous, but there are times a man needs to just be left alone. This was one of those times. After it was all over, I read the directions again and figured out there was this little tiny slide thing to slide up to get to the fuses. Well. Decided to follow directions, just in case. The fuses were just fine, but the lights still didn't work. Aggravating enough to make you want to swallow a whole bottle of cod liver oil pills.

There is a bit of history with me and my fingernails and toe nails. From way back when, bad things happened to them in ways I did not like one bit at all. I was forever stubbing my big toe as I played on the sidewalk there at 1018 Connecticut Avenue, and great day in the morning, how it would hurt. I had to sit there all by myself in the middle of the sidewalk, clutching my big toe, hauling it up somewheres near my chin so I could see the blood well out from underneath the nail like a slow flow of red lava. On occasion I made a bit of racket about it, not that anybody noticed or anything like that, except for Cedric, that great big nosy bull dog with a bashed in face and snorty nose. I hated that dog because he really didn't care. All he wanted to do was lick my face.

The worst time of all was when I was riding the English bike barefooted. Shoes were optional back in those days, and from time to time the disadvantage of this custom became clear. I really should-a had shoes on being as there was no chain guard, which mostly protects your pants leg from getting tangled up in the chain, which is not something you want to have happen. Trust me. This time it was not my pants leg that got chewed up. It was my big toe. Great day in the morning and oh, forever more. I shrieked and wailed like all get out. Cedric did not come to help me out. My mother came. She took me in the house, sat me down, and reached for the Watkins Lineament. I got a good dose of that on my toe that had most of the nail dangling off. I shrieked again, in a reactive fashion, just on account of the principle of the thing. Then she had an idea about that dangling toe nail. "We will have to get rid of that," she said. Whack. It was gone. I poured heart, soul, mind and strength into my vocal response, but for all my effort all I got was my big toe baptized with GermTrol. Holy Cow. That GermTrol came before Pine Sol was invented. It was for cleaning floors, for Pete's sake. Mother kept it for medicinal purposes, for such a long time that it got thick and green. It was potent enough to corrode the glass jar it was in. Enough already. How much can a body stand? I just hated it when that bottle came out.

And then there was the time that a cow bit my finger and popped the finger nail off of my left little finger. And the time I squashed my right little finger between a rock and a hard place, literally. I just have bad luck, is all I can say, lasting to this very day, as recent as Christmas tree decoration time last year.

As time went on, more and more of the little finger nail from Christmas pealed over, from port to starboard. And it would catch on the slightest little thing like bed sheets, shirts, britches pockets and ever darn thing within a radius of say, like 100 miles. I took matters in my own hands and tried to glue it down with Wacky Glue, or as my brother-in-law said, slightly insane glue. Didn't work. Bought Miracle Glue. That stuff is supposed to hold body parts together. I learned some time ago that Miracle Glue is faster, cheaper and less painful than stitches. Didn't work on binding finger nail to nail bed. So, I got out my miniature utility knife and against the protests of my wife, I set to work and trimmed it sort of like you would trim a cow's hoof. That helped a bit after it got done hurting.

But there was this stubborn patch that hung on in a very tenacious fashion, way over on the right side, from stern to bow. Finally the stern lifted a teeny-tiny little bit, but amidships and forward it hung on for dear life despite the fact it had to go some time. Tonight was the time. It had lifted enough that it just had to go. I knew there would be some pain involved, even though it was a little patch, but size has no correlation to pain. I got out my miniature box cutter and thought, well, maybe I could sort of pare it off by pushing things back a bit. That was not one of my better ideas.

Well, I decided to take matters in my own hand, so to speak. I grabbed ahold of that thing and gave a jank. Didn't get enough of a grab. Yielded nothing but pain and stiff neck muscles, and it stayed stuck, that miserable little sliver of a finger nail. I looked at it and thought deep thoughts. I thought long and hard. I thought about resolve and how I needed a lot of it right then. A good example of resolve came to mind and it had to do with those little piggies back there in Tennessee and how they would run under the electric fence, scot free until they got big enough for their ears to touch the wire. Lots of squealing, but no observable change in behavior, as they would stand back, eye things, and consider all the goodness on the other side of the fence, their porcine minds churning, deciding to do it all over again. You just knew that was what they were doing. They would study things, hunch up their backs, and start squealing right off the bat, and off they would go, so they wouldn't get caught by surprise and have to squeal in mid-stride and perhaps choke themselves while running and having to do an unplanned scream. The noise was necessary to get them through or under the wire while the sparks danced off their ears, and a week or two later, off their ears AND backs. Yes sir, resolution got them through, and it could do the same for me.

Well. I resolved to do what a man's gotta do. I got a firm hold on that thing again after rejecting the idea of employing a needle nose pliers. Took a deep breath, paused a moment to build up my courage, and then, and then...and then. Released my breath, and started all over again.

Since it was nobody in the house but me and the cats, I built up a full tank of determination, looked at what remained of that fingernail with a baleful gaze, grabbed ahold yet one more time, made sure I had a firm and unrelenting grip. Instead of squealing like those little pigs, I roared like Samson when he slew the Philistines with the jawbone of a donkey. I made that same kind of wide sweeping gesture, alls-a sudden.

There was reason for me to roar a supportive and encouraging roar, and it felt good to get it out of the way just before I really needed it. It was a proactive roar, so to speak. There are limits to pain when you do a heartfelt and sincere roar. It encourages and blesses action. Those pigs taught me that.

Now after I get a unit of blood transfused into my system, I should be right as rain. I do not refer to rain falling on my cheeks from the upstairs windows, so to speak. I don't even feel a whole lot faint anymore. The finger nail in its entirety is all gone now and a new one is

186

already on the way. It was a productive event.

Sometimes you just got to grab the bull by the horns, so they say, although I don't see any virtue in messing with bulls with horns. My position is sometime you got to grab ahold of something that needs to get done, knowing it will hurt like crazy, but it will be such an annoyance if it stays around. And besides, it won't hurt quite so bad if you do it yourself rather than having someone like your mother work at it. You make lots of noise and just do it, knowing that it will feel so good after it stops hurting.

A Cup on the Wall

We learned not to get attached to possessions back when I was growing up Mennonite in Knoxville, because we are just pilgrims here on this earth, and earthly things will not go with you into eternity. So what is the use of enjoying things in the present life, because in the end you will lose it all. And besides, if you get attached to things of this world, you will have trouble meeting Jesus in the air because there will be these strings attached from your body to material things and you will get to rise just so far and no more and it will be too late because you won't have a knife to cut the cords and the knots will be tied too hard to unravel.

Oh my. This was real serious business. I kind of wanted to have a few nice things anyhow but didn't want to get tied down by them because of the ramifications. These thoughts caused a lot of anxiety. We had to get creative to deal with this pressure.

One solution was to get stuff that was old and rotten but still had a bit of life left in it. If it was real ugly, like a rusty bike that nobody else would want, well, then you wouldn't get too attached to it. And as a bonus, you could exercise humility, which was a highly regarded virtue. It just didn't do to have special things just for you, because you would get all upset if somebody else exercised communal rights to what you mistakenly claimed as your own. Or if you did get something special for yourself, it should be real inexpensive, made out of cardboard or plastic, with a Bible verse printed on it. These are important growing up lessons so you can be a good Christian and have better reward in heaven.

Well, sir. One day my Sunday School teacher, quite innocently, nearly eliminated whatever chance I had of getting up to heaven. She gave me a special cup, a little cup, around a 6 ounce size, just the right size for my cocoa. I guess it was partially OK for me to have it, because it was real inexpensive, and had some words printed on it, religious words that I thought would be pleasing to Jesus. Those words were: "Thank you God for the birds that sing, Thank you God for everything." I loved my little cup, with the red pictures of playing children, but I tried not to get too attached to it because of the principle of the thing. It was best to leave it in the cabinet and not use it too much because of what it might lead to.

I know this is probably wrong of me, but I still have that cup, in its special place, and I am sort of attached to it. I can't bring myself to actually use it, you know, but I am joyful in a restrained kind of a way to still have it. I have happy thoughts about my cup, my SPECIAL cup. But I don't want to talk about it too much, because, well, you know why.

Even though I don't talk about my cup very much, I ponder cups in my heart and look at cups, mugs, steins, and tankards, and may God forgive me, I once in a while think they are sort of nice and special. I hope this is not a problem in the eternal scheme of things - I don't want to get into my cups too much or too deeply.

I did have occasion for some deep thinking about cups a long time ago when I was in a small fishing village up there in Massachusetts, north of the center of the universe, Boston. We stayed in a bed and breakfast and enjoyed ourselves a lot, walking around and looking at boats, window shopping and absorbing the general atmosphere of the village. Way early in the morning, long before I generally get up, I woke up and decided to take an early morning walk. I walked around and watched the sky turn from dark to purple to pink, smelled the tide coming in and whiffs of coffee, listened to the early morning sounds. The early morning dew settled on my face as I strolled around. It was a quiet and tranquil moment that lives in my memory yet. There was a restaurant open at that semi-dark hour of the morning, and I thought I would stroll in for a cup of tea and a bit of local color.

They didn't run me out, exactly. They were hospitable in a New England sort of way, I guess you could say. After a while a waitress came over, and I gathered she wanted to take my order, by virtue of the drooping of the nether lip, the squinting eye, the jutting hip, and the order pad in her hand. "Tea with sugar and lemon," I requested. She didn't say much, but she looked, and then she sauntered away. Maybe that is the way they do things there.

Eventually it came. In a plastic sort of insert that fit in a plastic shell device. Now I didn't really expect to be served my tea with a silver tea service, but being as there was a great collection of cups mounted on the wall, I figured that a reasonably nice mug would be not out of the realm of possibility. No, that was not the way it was to be. The plastic service was good enough for me, I guess, and it really didn't matter because it held the tea just fine.

Except that it did matter. It mattered a lot, because other people got their coffee or tea in a mug. In a variety of mugs, special mugs. I got to pondering on this thing, trying to figure out what was going on. There seemed to be a pattern. People would come in, and go to what I assumed was their regular spot. The waitress would look at them, go over to the wall, pick out their special mug, and fill it with coffee plus, coffee lite, coffee with or without white and/or sweet. Everybody except me had a cup on the wall. They belonged to the village, they were known. She smiled and talked with them, pleasant greetings were exchanged. It seemed a bit warmer over there where they sat. I was a stranger, just basically passing through on my way from Tennessee to somewheres else, so I just got my basic tea with no extras. The tea was warm - I could feel it through the thin plastic skin, but the atmosphere a bit cool where I was.

A great longing, a visceral wrench, a dampening behind my eye lids told me something deep was happening here. I was on the outside looking in. Yeah, I know we are supposed to be tent-dwelling pilgrims, with eyes looking forward to that heavenly city. But I got to live

191

in the here and now. Is it asking too much to have a place where they know you by name and keep your cup on the wall for you and make sure your cup will be there when you arrive? I am not talking about a silver cup, a goblet, a chalice, or the Holy Grail. It doesn't need to be fancy, but it doesn't need to be old and rotten, either. Just a bit more than your basic, generic cup. I am talking about a cup that may be a poor thing, but mine, a cup that is a symbol of place, time, and belonging. A place and a time when I am known by name, and there is a spot at the table for me.

I still have my little cup, a precious cup, and I have warm feelings every time I look at it. I bless my Sunday School teacher for giving it to me. I bless my mother for filling it up with cocoa. I bless my family for making a spot for me at our table. I bless friends who open their hearts and tables to me. So what if it is a temporary thing. It is still worth it. Say what you want. I think it is a good thing to be connected just a little bit to time and space, to know that you belong somewhere, and that people will be glad to see you stop by, and to enjoy things and people even before we get to that city that was not made by hands. Maybe we have to be pilgrims, but we can be happy ones. Maybe we can sort of act like we are in a heavenly city while we are waiting here below. Who says one has to end before the other one can start?

Tell you what. You can hang your cup on my wall and I will save a place for you as long as you need it. I can't figure out one good reason why that arrangement won't work, and as far as I am concerned, it can and will work.

That's Not the Way It Used to Be

I like old-timey music, the old bluegrass songs, and especially the Delta Blues from a long, long time ago. That old music sounds good to my ears because it reminds me of when I thought life was much simpler. They don't make music now-a-days that can hold a candle to the good stuff far as I am concerned. There is this one song that just aches for the past, and the chorus goes like this:

All the good times are past and gone,
All the good times are o'er.
All the good times are past and done,
Little darlin', don't you weep no more.

Now that is a song worth remembering and singing in mournful tones morning, noon, and night just to remind you that these here last days are perilous. We didn't sing that song in church, but we might as well have, because that was a central theme in our theology. After all, all you needed to do was to look around and read the signs of the times to know that. It helped if you believed in prophesy, because that just proved that things were bad already and were going to get a lot worse, so the best thing was to make time go backwards when things were a lot better, but you can't do that, so what are you going to do?

I tell you what you are going to do. You are going to remind yourself and everyone about you that things are bad and getting worse, and if only things were like they were way back when men had morals and stood on principle, not like the way it is now in the world, and how the church is crumbling around us, being destroyed from within because of influences from without.

Oh my. That is a heavy burden for a young boy growing up Mennonite in Knoxville to bear. I didn't have any past of my own that I could recall, so all I had to

193

ponder on was how they said it used to be, and that made my present miserable and the future even less appetizing. I mean really. If it used to be so good, and now we had to worry about destruction of all things good in the home and in the church, plus concerns about the economy going bust, the Communists taking over, and hiding under your school desk so the atom bomb wouldn't get you – well, how much worse could it get?

So our elders and betters worked real hard to keep us safe from doom and destruction by reminding us of these things on a regular basis, like at Sunday night preaching, revival meetings, and communion time. We got comforted by reminders that spiritual matters, especially at communion and foot washing time, could result in horrible outcomes if you did not do things properly. They used to have sweet fellowship at communion time, but now there was so much drift and you needed to make sure of things being lined up straight, and if they weren't, they needed to get straightened out pretty quick-like.

There was a way of doing things, and you best not mess around with these matters, because, well you know why. Of course – because that is not the way it used to be done.

Well, I tell you what. I am all grown up on the outside, but still a kid inside, and have a lot of catching up to do in the kid department. Things are different now and I will try to explain it to you. Tonight we had Maundy Thursday services. We didn't use to have a Maundy Thursday service because that is what Catholics did. Heck, we didn't even know what it was, other than it didn't make no sense. We did our foot washing on Sunday morning – none of this Thursday evening stuff. Except tonight it was different. First of all, we sat at round tables in the multi-purpose room. We ate soup and carrots and potato rolls. We drank water. We visited around the tables. We sang some songs and heard about how Jesus washed his disciples' feet and how it is a good idea for us to do the same.

Several teens from the youth group put on this mime about shining shoes for 10 cents, and this one guy had really bad shoes that were so muddy and all, and he didn't have 10 cents to pay, but he got his shoes scrubbed, washed, and shined anyhow, and got another pair of shoes in the bargain. They ended up by moving out among the folks and brushing off our shoes.

I sat way down in front, on the floor, so I could see. A crowd of kids, 10 years old and under sat there too and watched intently. They said I could sit down on the floor with them. Then we sang some more songs. The kids all gathered around a song book, trying to read the words and sing along. Since we believe in singing in parts in our church, they were getting confused because they couldn't hear the melody very well. So I did melody and they gathered around to do better. We didn't used to do it that way. You sat on a pew and stayed sitting except when you turned around and knelt at the church bench to pray and once in a great while standing to sing a song, and of course standing for the benediction. None of this moving around business to see the interesting stuff because first of all there wasn't any, and even if there was, you better not move so you could see it better. Kids weren't supposed to see or be seen. They were supposed to be patient and listen.

Then we were instructed that it was time for foot washing. And families could go together. And they did. There was cheerful talking and explanations. There was fellowship across generations. The kids were interested and wanted to be part of things. They got told that this is a way of showing how we want to serve other people, like when the youth group pretended to shine shoes. They were allowed to wash each other's feet. It started to make sense to me. It wasn't one bit scary, even for me. Holy cow. That is not the way it used to be.

Personally, I don't get into prophesy too much for the same reason that I don't watch horror movies. It just scares me too much. And I am not even convinced at all that things are getting worse and worse. I don't believe that all the good times are past and gone. Face it. The atom bomb didn't get us. The Communists didn't take over. The economy has its ups and downs, and for the most part it has been ups. The church has not collapsed. OK, OK, I hear it – yeah, none of these things happened, not yet, but one of these days, just you wait and see....

No sir. I've had enough of that and I am done with it.

You better believe it. What we did tonight was different. We sang:

> I come with joy, a child of God,
> Forgiven, loved, and free,
> The life of Jesus to recall
> His life laid down for me,

That is not an old-timey song, and far as I am concerned it is better than some of the old ones. It sounds just fine to my ears. Tonight we had thoughts of hope, like as if we had a future to be happy about. Oh boy, that's not the way it used to be, and I for one am glad.

"All the Good Times are Past and Gone," as sung by Ralph Stanley
"I come with joy to meet my Lord," Brian Wren
Text © 1971, Hope Publishing Co. All rights reserved. Used by permission.

What Goes Up

Me and my friend, Jimmy, down there west of Knoxville, enjoyed things that 12 year old boys used to enjoy doing back before there were electronic games and computers and stuff like that. We didn't even have a TV, which was probably just as good, because it gave more opportunity to run around with Jimmy. I am sure there were those that felt this was not the most edifying thing to do, but what do they know about it? They didn't know what Jimmy and I did. He did me a lot of good, because he knew everybody and wasn't afraid of anything. I didn't know nobody and was scared of everything, so Jimmy was a good influence in my way of thinking. I wanted to be a little more like him and a little less like me.

We did lots of things, like climbing trees. I mostly climbed in a restrained kind of way, hugging the tree trunk until the bark came off, and making sure the branch I stood on was stout before I let my weight down on it. Now Jimmy, he had a whole other method of tree climbing. It was straight up, both arms grabbing and both legs pumping, up, up, and away, until his head poked out the top of the tree. By that time, he was hanging on a trunk that was the size of your thumb, and that didn't provide a lot of support, but it didn't matter to Jimmy. He just twitched along, sort of like a red-winged blackbird hanging on a stem, enjoying himself. I couldn't drum up the courage to do that.

Part of the reason was my inborn cowardice and absolute allergy to pain. I didn't like the thought of broken bones and all the implications of climbing too high. There is a penalty to pay if you go up too high. This I knew for sure was a sin to be avoided because it was pride. That was when you thought you were better than you were, like when you reached higher than you should of. The other reason was because I read lots of Greek mythology when I was growing up Mennonite in Knoxville. That part of my life I kept hidden because it was not entirely proper to read mythology rather than the truth of the Scriptures. I did it anyhow. And the old Greeks and the Bible agreed that pride was not such a good idea.

While in junior high school, we read through Edith Hamilton's book on Greek mythology and I got to know those characters pretty good. From the ancient Greeks I learned it was best not to fly too high, because what goes up comes down, and the higher you go, the harder the thump.

Jimmy didn't read too much – he was too busy living. I doubt he ever took the Bible, Homer, or Virgil very seriously or even paid attention in school when we had to read Edith Hamilton's book, especially that story about these two guys, father and son, that were prisoners on this island and wanted to get away. They figured out if they took wax and stuck feathers in it and strapped this contraption on their arms, they could fly away like a bird. And it worked, until the one flew too high, and the sun melted the wax and down he went with such a thump in the sea he never came up again. That is what happens when you overreach. It is called hubris and the Greek gods didn't like that one little bit at all. They would get you and cause you to fall down real hard.

There seemed to be laws of gravity, theology, and mythology at work here, and this kept me from taking risks. But Jimmy, he didn't know about these things so he up and did what he wanted to without concerns about hubris. That caused me to wonder about things, and urged me to try out Jimmy's approach. So I took to climbing high, with my throat constricted and my back all itchy.

Then he got to climbing up real skinny trees, almost too skinny to climb, and kicking out while holding on and riding the tree town to the ground in a graceful arc. Whoo-ee. That was fun. It was so much fun we did it over and over again and Robert Frost wrote a poem about it.

There was this one time we went to see Dickie, over there on Hardin Valley Road, to climb his tree. It was a great big pine tree, on the other side of a bob war fence. There was a gate in the fence to get to the tree, but why bother with opening a gate when you can jump the fence. Hop, hop, like two deer, over went Jimmy and Dickie straight to the tree. For my part it was run, think about this thing, hop, but just an inch too short so both toes snagged on the wire. What went up came down in a most unpleasant fashion. I would have broken both arms had I not been so slow of reaction time, so I didn't get my hands in front of me in time. I just went nose first into that hard clay Tennessee soil. It raised a huge cloud of dust which hid my embarrassment while I disentangled myself and staggered on.

That day I didn't climb very high in the tree. But Jimmy and Dickie did. They went up high as the sky, and Jimmy told Dickie about riding trees to the ground. Dickie, he was way up there, and took Jimmy's advice. He grabbed the trunk where it was real skinny, held on for dear life, and kicked out for the ride of his life.

It very nearly was the ride of his death, because the tree had limited flexibility the thicker the trunk got. As the skinny part bent over, it got to the point where there was no more bending. It snapped. Dickie came down, crashing through 40 feet of branches, with a startled look on his face. He hit the ground with an awful sound, sort of like a semi-wet thwack, accompanied by a high-pitched wheeze. He just stayed there in a crumbled heap on the ground and liked to scared me and Jimmy to death. By the time we got to him, he was sitting up, gasping for air. At least he wasn't dead.

That put the damper on things for that day. But not for long.

Jimmy got the idea of swinging from tree to tree up there in Mr. Smith's woods. There was this pine thicket where the trees were close, and we decided to make like monkeys and swing from tree to tree for as long as the trees lasted. If you jumped hard enough, you would make it to the next branch. After a while you got enough pine rosin all over you so you would stick better. I landed mostly OK, but Jimmy misjudged things one time and

199

missed his branch. He went slipping and sliding, real smoothly, from one branch to the other until he stuck. His eyes were pretty big from excitement when he got to a good place, and he scrambled right back up again. We even went tree swinging one winter day when the trees were snow and ice covered. Now you talk about slipping and sliding. We did a lot of it that day, but got from one side to the other without serious mishap. We got cold from the weather, but all warmed up because of the danger. I was scared, but did it anyway, and it was the thrill of victory that kept me going. Yes sir, me and Jimmy flew pretty high that day. Whenever I see a squirrel going from one tree to another, I think, huh, that ain't nothing. Me and Jimmy used to do that a lot.

When I was 16, I went up to the woods all by myself. By that time I had been away from home a year, lost contact with Jimmy. I wanted to recapture the freedom and joy I had on that winter day, so I tried to swing from tree to tree all by myself. It wasn't fun anymore. Jimmy wasn't there. I missed him and the good times we had together. The loss was almost too great to bear. I was growing up and it was not reasonable to do silly things like climbing trees and doing needless risk taking. Nobody said that exactly, but I knew how things went.

You can leave home, but you can't come back in the same way. Things change. You can't have unbridled freedom and joy anymore. The weight of adulthood starts to hang on, and for me it felt like Saul's armor, but I didn't have the balls to say, "Phooey with this. I am not going to wear this. I can take on the grown up giants in my own way." But, I took it on and tried to adjust to forms and shapes that were expected of me. Maybe that is the way it had to be.

But then, I had to think of that guy that flew too close to the sun and got punished for it because the gods didn't like his excessive pride, the hubris that was an offense to them. So getting lifted up with pride wasn't a good idea. But on the other hand, I wondered if there was a curse upon humans when they didn't fly high enough, when their armor kept them heavily grounded. Never got an answer to that question. I even called up this guy in Princeton Seminary, who stayed on to get his doctorate in Greek Classics. I asked him if there was a curse in Greek mythology for flying too low. "Why are you asking that question," he said. "I never heard of anything like that."

Seemed to me like there should have been more, but end of discussion. I still don't have an answer. What goes up must come down, but what if it never goes up in the first place?

"Tee-Hee, Don't Hurt"

I remember all but of my grade school teachers back when I was growing up Mennonite in Knoxville and most of my high school teachers. I can recall many of them by name and remember relationships with them. Fortunately I have a few memorable teachers whose impact on my life was of the positive nature. But there was this one teacher - oh boy. It was my first grade teacher, and I can't even remember her name.

It wasn't exactly my first grade teacher, precisely. There were two of them. The first one was a beautiful, nurturing teacher and I fell in love with her. She was so sweet and kind to us. I wanted to be just like her when I grew up. Well, apparently she gave her heart to another person, because her belly started to get big and bigger. And then the awful day when she announced to us that she would not be with us the rest of the year because she had a baby in her belly that was going to come out and she would have to take care of it. I was so confused by that. I thought she liked us and would want to be with us. She said we were special children, and now she was leaving us. My belly felt small and like it was hungry.

It was confusing - how did that baby get in her belly in the first place? And why did it have to happen if it took her away from us? You have these questions, but somehow you know some of these things are Not Talked About.

And - who would teach us next? Would she be pretty and kind? Would she be as sweet as our real teacher?

Well, we got our answer, and the answer was NO. I should of been prepared for this because most of my questions got the answer of NO but still it was a shock to see this strange woman come into the classroom the next day.

She was not pretty. She was not kind. She was old and mean. She had this frazzled air about her, like she was upset about having to get up in the morning. Having to handle a roomful of first-graders most likely did not help her become more settled. I don't think she liked being there with us.

She had hair all over her head. She stooped frontwards and twisted sidewards at the same time. She had these long dresses that had flowers on them and lots of buttons. Her collar was made out of lace. She had lots of wrinkles on her face and not many smiles. She must have taught first graders for a million years and regretted every one of them. Maybe she should have been a librarian.

She wanted the class to be orderly, but we were all disordered. Our real teacher left us and this other woman came into our world and that simply was not OK. We were sad, and she was sad, about the same thing, sort of. We were sad because she was there instead of our teacher, and she was sad because she had to be there.

Most of us were sad in silence, which was satisfactory to our unreal teacher. But Johnny - he wasn't content to be quiet about his pain. He had a different way of dealing with his distress. He would misbehave in his own ways, like talking in rest time, laughing in reading time, playing in arithmetic time, and not paying attention in paying attention time. This created amusement for us and frustration for the substitute teacher. We just waited to see what would happen next, even though after a while we knew pretty well what would happen next.

Oh, that teacher would get bent out of shape. I mean really bent out of shape, and not figuratively. It was a bodily style of bent out of shape. She bent and twisted in unnatural positions. "Oh, Johnny," she whined. "You should be good."

Johnny didn't care. He didn't want to be good. He wanted to be who and what he was. Who and what he was - well, these things were not satisfactory to Teacher. She was clear and specific about it. This was funny to us because we thought Johnny was just fine the way he was.

Johnny thought the same thing, because he was not interested in doing better, despite her pleas for positive choices. Instead of telling the teacher how much he appreciated her good efforts on his behalf, he would just laugh and keep on going, being his own self anyhow.

Then the big guns would roll out. This type of defiance needed to be quelled immediately. It had to be nipped in the bud so Johnny wouldn't grow up to be a bank robber or a jail bird, which is the natural consequence of fooling around in first grade. Anybody who went to Lonsdale Elementary School knew that.

Teacher went to her desk and got the wooden ruler. She held it upright in her right hand like a witch's wand, and moved forward toward Johnny's desk in a meaningful way. We all gasped in unison, in a spirit of horror and sympathy. But once the ruler was raised, there was no turning back. Like they say in theater, if the gun is drawn, it must be fired.

And the ruler was applied; it measured out punishment. Teacher grabbed Johnny's fingers and twisted the hand palm up. Then she bent the fingers in the opposite direction that they normally bent until the palm was nice and flat and taut as a drum skin.

Johnny leaned forward in anticipation, with great interest in what was going to happen next. With that ruler, Teacher went tippy-tip-tip on his hand.

Johnny just laughed about it. "Tee-hee," he smirked. "Don't hurt." Once again, bent palm, and this time rat-a-tat-tat with the ruler. "Tee-hee, don't hurt," said Johnny, while we were wide eyed with tension.

Teacher also had some tension. Things were not going like they were supposed to. Kids were supposed to behave, and if they didn't, they were to get punished. And getting punished was not a laughing matter. No sir, not at all. Getting punished was supposed to make you submit and behave better.

This time, with grim determination and facial expression, Teacher twisted into a genuine human pretzel, and went to work. Ruler now made a quicker, whack-a-whack-a-whack kind of sound. But Johnny, he did not wince nor cry aloud. He refused to give in or give up.

With a grimace thinly covered with a grin, eyes crinkling and shining with unshed tears, he looked Teacher straight in the eye and said, yet once again, "Tee-hee, don't hurt."

Tell you the truth. I don't know what happened next, exactly. I do know Teacher eventually gave up, and Johnny triumphed, even as he held his hand under the desk. He stood up to ever what she could do to him. He took it and just laughed about it.

Johnny, how many years has it been since we were in first grade? I doubt you remember me. I remember you, even though I forgot the names of both our first grade teachers. You were a good example of bearing up under adversity. You showed me that the worst isn't so bad, if you can look it straight in the eye and say, "Tee-hee, don't hurt." It can hurt like all get out, but just don't show it. Don't give troubles the pleasure perceiving your pain. By doggies, wear them out with outright doggedness, sheer determination, and bold defiance.

Way to go, Johnny, and may your tribe increase.

I Shouldn't Of Laughed

Mr. Stanley was my 8th grade science teacher, and it was his first year of teaching. Looking back on it, he did a pretty good job, near as I can tell, being as he looked strong and was given to unnecessary words, but at the time we just saw him as fresh meat. We had good intentions in mind. We wanted him to succeed and become an outstanding teacher, to learn patience, and to excel in classroom management. As I recall, he did not see it that way, and didn't appreciate our efforts just a whole lot.

When I say, "we," it was not just other students. It includes me, sorry to say. I was right in the thick of things, testing the limits, and working hard to forget who I was. I did not want to remember that I was growing up Mennonite in Knoxville and had a last name of Yoder. My dad often spoke about a good name being more precious than silver or gold, but at the time, that was not high on my list of priorities, especially when I was away from home and church and stuff like that.

Mr. Stanley, I am sure, wished that certain students would remember who they were, and that they would choose to work for a good name and loving favor rather than acting like they were East Tennessee 8th graders. He didn't put it that way, exactly, but I could sort of read between the lines.

There was this one unruly day when some of us were misbehaving and not heeding Mr. Stanley's warnings to tighten up. His temper rose and so did his voice. He said we had better stop messing around. Everything got quiet for a little bit, but being as I was half-way back the room, there was no reason to take things personally.

I yukked it up a bit, thinking I was well hidden. Well, next think I knew, there stood Mr. Stanley right by my desk. Alls-a sudden I was standing out in the hall with a visibly upset teacher trembling before me. "Were you laughing at me," he demanded.

I heard that liars go to hell, and I didn't want to go there sometime in the future when the trumpet sounded, but if I didn't lie, terrible things would happen now.

"N-n-n-o, I waddn't," I said, while my eternal fate was being mapped out for me. The immediate future didn't look very promising either. "Looked like you were laughing," he said, voice full of foreboding.

I thought very quickly. How to wiggle out of this one? Laughing at a bad time is not funny, and if things are not funny then you can't be laughing, now can you? Laughing involves going haw-haw-haw in a merry way, which is what laughing is. I wasn't going haw, haw, haw, exactly. It was more of a yuk-yuk-yuk, and nobody else was laughing so it wasn't funny and there you go. I wasn't laughing.

"No, Mr. Stanley, believe me. I wasn't laughing." I knew there were very bad things in store for me. The gaping jaws of destruction were just about to clamp down on me. God was recording each word and Mr. Long, the principal, his office was not so very far away. This was not a good thing. Mr. Long believed in paddling, so a little evasion seemed to be a good thing at the time.

Mr. Stanley raised his arm, and my knees got weak. If I looked as scared as I felt, it would have been a horrible sight, sort of like a skeleton or something like that. He did not hit me. He leaned himself against the wall, with his hand near my head. He probably needed to hit me.

But he didn't. He was made of stern stuff. He muttered a few sentiments, something like "you better not ever again" or something like that, and back in the deathly quiet classroom I went.

"What did he do," Jimmy and them demanded after class. "Aw, nuttin," I replied. "He just talked. That was all."

Sorry to say, but that was not the last time I had troubles in the laughing department. Seems like that habit followed me throughout life.

Take for instance. My neighbors have these two dogs and they can be rather snarly at times. And to make matters worse, they treat my lawn like their personal savings and loan department, at least half ways like one. They always make deposits but never make withdrawals. I would be glad to give them interest, but it doesn't work that way. I don't like those dogs very much. They should stay over on their side of the line and pee against his trees and poop in his lawn. He has some trees, big ones, and a nice lawn. That should meet their needs quite well.

Well, my neighbor wanted to take down this one great big old Silver Maple tree, and I was over helping him out. There was a whole big bunch of guys there, working, talking, and drinking beer. I did two of the three. This guy Cork kept a cigar burning which was not a problem for me as I sort of like the smell of a cigar outside the house. Me and Cork were gathering together branches and hauling them to the truck. I looked over and here was Cork all bent over a pile of branches. My neighbor was down on his knees. Someone called out, "Hey, did you lose your contact lens?" "Something like that," he replied, and they kept on looking.

Well, me, wanting to be helpful and all, I walked over and asked what it was we were looking for. "Aw, Cork, he lost his see-gar," said my neighbor. So three of us pawed through the twigs and branches, Cork a bit more intensely than I. "Cork," I said, "be careful that you pick up the cigar rather than a dog turd."

The young folks thought this was funny. I laughed along with those who were laughing. Cork, he didn't laugh. He is the strong silent type and was very thoughtful when he found that cigar.

I shouldn't of laughed, but I did. That cigar sticking out of his mouth - well, it made me think thoughts.

I don't mind the silent types, or the strong types, but when you put them both together, there may be some ramifications in certain circumstances.

I know that now.

An Inconvenient Truth

Back when I was growing up Mennonite in Knoxville, there were certain expectations about life and play. You were supposed to live virtuously and play properly. That is the way it is supposed to be. Boom. There you got it. Whether something was fun did not enter into the equation at a very high level, at least in my experience, because many of the things I thought were fun were neither proper nor virtuous.

Before I was ten years old, I developed a fascination with guns, even though I knew this was improper and was not virtuous. Cowboys and Indians was not a good game to play because it involved shooting. It was hard to play Cowboys and Indians without shooting, because that eliminated an essential component. What is the fun if you can't shoot? Even pretend shooting with a stick or your finger was forbidden.

We got around the No Guns Allowed Ruling in creative ways. You can take a rubber band, hook it on your pointer finger, pull it back, and if you do things just right, you can shoot it across the room and whack somebody. If you didn't get it right, it would back fire right into your face; it would shoot backwards. Man, that smarted. Or you could take a clothes pin apart, tape the slanted ends together and use the spring in a special way to shoot a wad of paper, a corn kernel, or a match. It if was a good shot, you could send things away far over Jordan. With a match you might have the added pleasure of a miniature flaming projectile. An L-shaped piece of wood could be rigged up with a clothes pin to shoot rubber bands. That eliminated the back firing problem and increased accuracy. We tried to do these things in secret because of The Ruling.

But there was this one time when me and my brother ventured into forbidden territory. First we saved our pennies until we had 39 cents plus tax, and we snuck down Johnson Street to the variety store and made a covert purchase of wee tiny, single fire cap guns, one little gun per little boy. We just had to have them. They had these little holsters, and you could get a roll of caps, stick a cap under the hammer, click the trigger, and CRACK - a small burst of flame and a magical whiff of gun smoke. It was so satisfying.

Oh, man, it don't get any better than that. The guilty joy of keeping things a secret! We made real sure Mother didn't find out. This was one of the things she did not need to know about. We did not want her to carry a burden on our account, you know.

Back in those days we were told over and over again, "Be sure your sins will find you out." They said that at home, they said it at school. They said it everywhere, both as a warning and as a reproach. I didn't like that saying at all. It seemed so absolute, and there ought to be a little flexibility here.

That is why we hid our little guns very carefully when we weren't using them back in the alley. We found a very good and safe place to keep them. Buried under our underwear in the clothes drawer. Nobody would go looking there. Nobody was supposed to go snooping in our drawers. No self-respecting person would go pawing through our underwear.

Well. We forgot a crucial detail that you already figured out, I am sure. Mothers reserve the right to go looking where you don't want them to. It wasn't very many days until Mother called us for a little conversation. It was brief and to the point. "Boys," she said. "Look what I found. Where did you get these things? I am very disappointed."

Oh my. We were found out. It felt like we were carrying the guilt and shame of the whole universe on our little weak shoulders. Little things get so heavy and it

212

weighs the shoulders down. The shoulders sag, as well as the eye lids and the lower lip.

That saying about your sins finding you out was an inconvenient truth. And there were so many sayings like that. After a while you get suspicious about truth - it is something to be avoided because it is such bad news, and gets in the way of happy living.

Now, if I could make my own universe, I would do things just a bit differently. Instead of having sayings like "Be Sure Your Sins Will Find You Out" as the headlines on the daily paper, I would make them a footnote on the stock market report. Instead of making the universe focus on unpleasant truths, I would make it convenient for pleasant truths to be a bit more front and center.

Maybe the truth of the matter is that I was a kid who wanted to have fun with a little cap pistol - that is all. It didn't mean I wanted to grow up and make shooting people my life's vocation. In the balance of life, I bet I have a lot more good qualities than bad, even though it seemed inconvenient to acknowledge this truth.

Confession Time

That beady-eyed, twitchy 9th grade math teacher there at Karns High School provided me with no end of sporting pleasure. Now, most of the people in my area took to rifles, shot guns, fishing rods, hot rods, or knives for blood sport. Being as I was a Mennonite growing up in Knoxville, fishing was the only option open to me, and that on a limited basis. All I had left in the sporting department, offensively speaking, were words and undercover maliciousness. That seemed to work pretty well for me. Mr. Potter was such a convenient and enjoyable target.

My parents taught me to be kind to animals and to the less fortunate. The first part worked pretty well, but when it came to some of the less fortunate, I was kindness challenged. Especially in 9th and 10th grades when I had Mr. Potter as math teacher. He was a sight. He was one of the less fortunate.

To begin with, his eyes were wild and shifty. He was all disheveled, both with his hair and his suits. He had these mannerisms that were revolting. For example, if he couldn't find an eraser, he would grab the cuff on the sleeve of his rumpled jacket and use the length of his fore arm to erase the chalkboard. That crumpled jacket sleeve got even dirtier with chalk dust. He would spit when he talked and that was so unpleasant, especially when he came by your desk to explain a math problem. "You take this and add it to that and take and multiply by this here there you got it." There were showers of non-blessings with each "s" and "th" sound. He wasn't a good explainer at all. The spit got in the way, especially the time he explained from the side and a glob fired straight from his lips to behind my glasses and glanced off my eyeball. "One-a these days," I thought.

Now, what is a fellow to do? I was not real inclined to turn the other eyeball. There has to be revenge for things like this.

Well, I learned his weak points. Once in a while, on rare occasions, there would be quietness in the room. One of us would start humming a steady, low hum, real quiet-like, and another, and another, a whole room full of studious boys humming until the whole room was filled with Zen humming.

Mr. Potter, he would look around like something was tickling his protruding ear hairs. He would rub his ear with his little finger or take a pencil, stick the eraser end in his ear, wrench it around, pull it out, and examine the results. Then he would shake his head and move over to the window, throw up the sash, and look out for the airplanes, only to discover the sound was coming from behind him. "HYEAR!" he would roar when all of him got back inside, and then it was quiet no more.

Sometimes when it was nice and quiet, one of the boys, probably Matt, in a real high voice, would sing out a segment from one of the Chuck Wagon Gang songs, "I've found a hiiiiding place," and Mr. Potter would roar out, "WHUR?" That meant where was this latest indignity coming from. He never found out.

Mr. Potter and Matt behaved like two tom cats. Matt would strut up to him, say something provocative, and Mr. Potter would say, "Matt. Matt. Matt!" Until both were bristling real good and Mr. Potter would say, "Matt! Do you wont me to kick you whur it hurts?" Matt would say, "Heh heh heh heh," and poor Mr. Potter would quiver something awful. And it was so much fun to watch this going on.

But the worst thing was to call out "Mary Parks." I never learned why, but ever time, Mr. Potter would roar out "HEY!" which being interpreted meant do it again. That was so much fun. We even took to sending up a decoy to the desk to ask for help with a math question, and while he was distracted, boys would walk up to the blackboard, one by one, and print M-A-R-Y P-A-R-K-S in nice big letters and when he would finally turn around, he would roar "HEY!"

216

It was never clear if "Mary Parks" was a name or a sentence. Could have been both. In our gentle fashion we sought clarification, but all we got from him was shuffling around and a mutter of "They was never anything between of us. We was just friends." It seemed like there was a bit more than that. This whole situation was ambiguous, both grammatically and morally, and we just wanted to make sure of what we were dealing with.

Even though I was in the middle of baiting Mr. Potter on a very consistent basis, there were times I wished for better self-control because of the principle of being a witness, and letting my light shine. What an awful situation, because if I didn't behave in a godly fashion, there would be trouble twice a year at Communion time, to say nothing about when the Great Rapture came. I would get left behind and it would be forever too late.

I knew all about these things, being as I heard about them on a constant basis. Geographically, Knoxville was not the buckle on the Bible Belt, but even there we all knew about, and feared the Second Coming, unless you had eternal security. Mennonites don't have eternal security. That is why we needed to behave ourselves.

But even good behavior can have an evil side. Mr. Potter would sometimes creep up to a student to ask about a relative who used to be one of his students. "Are they mar-ret?" Then he would grin that ghastly grin, and continue, "Do they have any lit-luns?" I wanted to be friendly, you see, so one day when he sauntered past, I asked him. "Hey, Mr. Potter, are you married?" He seemed to be a bit awkward with this question. His shoulders twitched, his eyes darted back and forth, and foam gathered at the corners of his mouth. "Wall, I guess so," he finally choked out. "You got any lit-luns?" I continued. "HEY, Yoder. HYEAR." roared Mr. Potter.

Honestly, I tried real hard to be a good witness to Mr. Potter and my classmates, especially at Communion time when my conscience was quickened. I would try to apologize for my behavior and all he would say was

"Huhhhn. Huhhhn. We'll see 'bout that." This one time I didn't even get the words out on account of I leaned on his desk top waiting for courage, quite forgetting that the top of his desk was just a loose collection of 1x4 slats. I was out on the edge and alls-a sudden, this 1x4 flipped up in the air, scattering his junky piles of paper and just that quick whacked back down. "WHACK!" went the board and Mr. Potter's eyebrows went up, along with his voice. "HYAR!" roared Mr. Potter, and I slunk back to my desk, unforgiven, feeling awful, and secretly amused. I figured my good intentions would get me through Communion time that year.

After many years I must confess something. Why did I behave so miserably towards Mr. Potter? Just because it was fun at the time is no excuse for treating him like I did. I have a few regrets, most likely not enough. And how am I supposed to get forgiven if I am not 100% remorseful? Some folks believe that you are forgiven right from the get-go, long before you were born, long before you had the chance to need forgiveness. I don't know about that. Seems a bit fishy to me. Mennonites don't believe in that at all. Under the best circumstances, forgiveness is sort of a temporary condition. This thing of forgiving and forgetting does not exist. What you really need is 100% remorse 100% of the time, a whole bagful of remorse to collect and carry around. Forgiveness means being easy on sin, and being easy on sin is not acceptable. Confession is good for you, but getting forgiven is quite another matter.

And while the mood is upon me, I must also confess that I still do not know if "Mary Parks" was a name or a sentence.

On Louisiana Avenue

As I flew over the handle bars of the bicycle, I just knew there was a world of hurt waiting for me, and that I wouldn't need to wait too long before that world would encircle me with surges of regret and pain.

Actually, the realm of regret was reached long before I hit the pavement. I recalled that I was in forbidden territory, as I crossed Johnson Street to get to Louisiana Avenue, and not only crossed Johnson Street, but rode down it for a block. This was a definite no-no. We were allowed to walk across Johnson Street, but not ride across because it was unnecessary and we might get hit by a car if we were on a bicycle.

That was just one avenue for regretful thoughts. Another was that I was riding my brother's bicycle, an English bike, with narrow tires and three gears. Never mind that I didn't have a bike to ride of my own, and of course HE had the bike, and didn't ever knowingly share, like I would have done if the situation were reversed and all. I just wasn't allowed. Not being allowed doesn't mean you don't do it. It means make sure you don't get caught, which is a good reason to cross Johnson Street and go down Louisiana Avenue, so you aren't seen doing forbidden things. But I was there, without permission and against the rules.

To my shame and sorrow, I must admit that my motivations for going down Louisiana Avenue were not purely honorable. True, the li-b'ary was down at the end of the avenue, but before that was the fire house, and that was my true destination. Even though I was a Mennonite growing up in Knoxville, and should have known better, I didn't exactly do better a whole lot of the time and this was one of those times. You see, there were so many interesting things to see at the fire house. The fire engines, the slide down pole, the hose tower and stuff like that. The firemen showed me these things. They explained things of interest, like you had to fasten the hose very firmly to the pump and hold on to the nozzle

219

real tight because of pressure. And how every time the hoses got wet, you need to loop them up and down in the hose tower and dry them out, ever single time, because if you don't, the hoses will rot, and you don't want that to happen because then the hose will pop when the pressure goes on and you won't get the fire out that way.

Being as it was a fire house, there were some other things there to see, but the firemen didn't explain those things to me. It was left up to me to draw my own conclusions. I knew I was being naughty, but my need for extracurricular continuing education pressed hard upon me. I refer to lessons relating to anatomy and physiology, and they had these illustrated, paperback manuals that were of such interest. I was only eight years old, but inquiring minds want to know. And face it, those manuals, which some would call dirty magazines, had good articles in them, or so I heard. Can't say as I paid a lot of attention to the articles. When it came to text, I was mostly interested in the Dr. Seuss books, such as Bartholomew and the Oobleck from the li-b'ary next door. But Dr. Seuss' pictures weren't as attractive to me compared to what I found next door on the front porch of the fire hall.

And, there were lots of other things to think about while I was still airborne.

I had to think about how smooth the asphalt was on Louisiana Avenue, not bumpy like it was on Connecticut Avenue. You could ride real fast on that stuff. And I remembered seeing that manhole cover, and how it was above the surface of the street, enough to be of concern. I worked real hard to steer around it, but the more I concentrated on missing that stupid thing, the more I went straight for it. This was not fair. Why on earth would I wind up hitting the very thing I sincerely wanted to avoid? I knew the consequences would be disastrous, and they were.

I hit that manhole cover dead center. The front wheel jerked and twisted to the left and overboard I went, landing hard on Louisiana Avenue, bounced along four or five times like a skipper rock across the surface of a pond, leaving patches of pants and skin along the way. I howled like a fire whistle, real loud and piercing. I brayed like a donkey. My pain was sounded abroad like Gabriel blowing his trumpet on the Last Day. That was just the physical pain part.

The other, more serious pain set in when I gathered together what was left of me and looked at the bike. That front wheel was turned all around backwards. The handle bars pointed forwards like horns on a cow. Oh no, what will my brother say now? I had to get things straightened out, but the wheel was stuck somehow on the frame. I tugged and tugged. No use. It was STUCK.

No longer was I concerned about being wounded and bleeding. I was seriously pleading for a solution. To call for help, human or divine, I set up another heart-rending siren of sorrow, very loud, that was surely heard up and down Louisiana Avenue, and probably in heaven as well, all to no avail. People sat on the front porch and watched. They did not come to help out. Jesus did not come to help out, either. There I was, inconsolable and alone. If anything was to be, it was up to me. Things just had to get turned around before I went home.

Buddy, I tell you what. Desperate times call for desperate measures. A non-rational resolution came to me out of my panic and dread of future retribution. I seized those cow horns of handle bars, jerked and tugged, and with the surge of adrenaline that helps little people do big things, I cut loose with a roar and a massive heave. That handle bar, and the wheel, became unstuck and swung around. There were some scratches on the bike, but never mind about them. They could have been there before all of this happened.

After my tears dried up, and my quivering body became a bit more governable, I did not continue to the li-b'ary via the fire house. No, I went home. Not for forgiveness, because these things are best not talked about. I just wanted a quiet place, like up in the attic, where I could be all alone and recover, and then come down and be all nonchalant and everything.

Far as I know, nobody but me ever knew what happened that day on Louisiana Avenue. But I remember it. And I have had many, many years to think about this thing. Not about why I was on Louisiana Avenue, or why I rode across Johnson Street, or why I went to the fire house when I sort of indicated that I wanted to go to the li-b'ary. No, none of those things confuse me a whole lot. That is simple to figure out, based on awareness of human development and biology. The real imponderable is that elevated manhole cover. I knew it was there. I knew it meant trouble. I knew if I hit it, disaster would surely come. Seriously, I worked so hard to steer around it, and the harder I worked on avoiding it, the worse it got. I headed right to where I didn't want to go. I headed right where I was looking. My attention was focused on that clear and present danger. And I hit the very thing I did not want to hit, dead center, a catastrophic bull's eye.

I came to the conclusion, much later on about this. There must have been a principle involved, and I figured it out when I did the Motorcycle Safety Foundation's Basic Rider's Course. There they taught us a good lesson. They said if you come upon an obstacle you don't want to hit, don't look at it. Look at where you want to go, instead of where you don't want to go, because your cycle goes right where your eyes are looking. This is not just an idea. It is true.

Maybe I could have saved myself a lot of grief there on Louisiana Avenue that day, and later on in many different situations and locations, if I would have paid less attention to what I should avoid and more attention to the best way around it.

Precious Jewels

There is this curious thing about learning things in church if you happened to grow up Mennonite in Knoxville. I am not talking about what part of the Bible you learn things from. No, it is specific places that I am talking about. That has a huge bearing on what you learn when you are 5 years old. What you learned sort of depended on the physical spot you were in at a particular time, you know, learning things that really make you wonder, things that can help you feel good, and things that help you feel afraid, morning, noon, and night.

When we were with Ruth Byler in children's meetings in the basement of the Knoxville Mennonite Mission, we sang about children being special. We sang:

When He cometh, when he cometh, to take up his jewels,
All his jewels, precious jewels, His loved and his own.
Like the stars of the morning, His bright crown adorning,
They shall shine in their beauty, Bright gems for his
crown.

Down in the basement, you could sing that song and be comforted by it. We sang that with gusto and confidence because Ruth Byler sang it with us, and smiled, and helped us believe we were special. We were so special that we got to hear missionary stories and Bible stories, we got to do activities and fun stuff, we got to tell our stories and to pray about things that are important to kids down there in the basement.

Upstairs we learned about other things, like the Age of Accountability. We learned all about sin and how it would sneak up on you, and the consequences of giving in to it were just terrible, what with the first and last books of the Bible. Genesis told us how sin got into the world and Revelation told us what was going to happen to us on account of sin. It was Eve's fault. She caused Adam to sin. Then Adam and Eve had kids and caused them to sin also. That is how sin got infectious and you got it just

223

because you were born. You couldn't do anything about it. You got to be sinful without knowing what happened. And the consequences – oh boy. Revelation explained it clearly, much too clearly for my tastes. Don't want to go there because it was just too horrible to think about, except I did think about it. All the time, morning, noon, and night. Especially at night.

And of course, in my way of thinking it was hard to be upstairs and downstairs in the same church house. I kindly wanted it to be a rancher kind of a building where things were a bit more sensible, but that is not the way it was supposed to be, I guess. I sat upstairs and then I sat downstairs and tried to put these things together.

Along about 5 or 6 years of age, you began to if wonder if you were such a precious jewel after all. When He cometh, He will take up the precious jewels, you know, the girls mostly, the nice ones who memorized their Bible verses and sat quietly in upstairs times. The rest of us cracked and dim jewels, you know, the Cracker Jacks variety, would not be picked out of the jewel basket and be chosen to be in His crown. We would get left behind during The Rapture because of Genesis and Revelation and all.

Downstairs we talked about moral dilemmas and theological considerations. There were shades of interpretations. We learned that the Bible says, "Children, obey your parents in the Lord." Me and some of the others wondered if there was some wiggle room there. Why was that In The Lord part there? What did that mean? Now, Ruth Byler, she thought it was a good question since we asked it. Are children supposed to obey their parents each and every single time, say for instance, if your parents told you to go out and steal something? You aren't supposed to steal but you are supposed to obey your parents. Both ideas are in the Bible, right there in the Ten Commandments. What if your parents aren't Christian? How are you supposed to obey them in the Lord if they aren't Christians? Ruth Byler gently reminded us that our parents wouldn't put us in that sort of bind, but we still wanted an answer to the What If. So we kept talking about it, and came to a conclusion that it was up to us to be faithful to God's commandments, and we would just have to work it out the best way we could. The idea was both to obey and not to steal. That is the way God wanted it to be. I could deal with that.

Upstairs, things were a bit more defined. We got reminded about sin, separation, salvation and how you better start doing better or else. Not much opportunity to figure stuff out on account of by the time questions got upstairs, they were already figured out. The preacher, bless his heart, was concerned about these matters, and earnestly pled with us to turn from our sinful ways. "Oh, sinner man," he would say. "Oh, sinner woman. Oh, sinner boy. Oh, sinner girl." Somehow, I felt included in that list, and felt like I ought to do something to get excluded, but didn't have an idea what to do about it. Once in a while during this recitation, I snuck a look in an effort to figure out which Sinner Man or Sinner Woman was being singled out and what the preacher knew about them that I didn't. Mostly I racked my brain trying to figure out what I had done to deserve the entire rumpus.

Downstairs we experienced being precious jewels; upstairs it sounded like we were not so precious after all. Downstairs, we were safe. Upstairs we needed to get saved. That got me all mixed up, and I got suspicious about jewels in general, and worried about being precious in His sight.

Well, now. If I would have my druthers, I would change things around a little bit. I would not try to speed up the Age of Accountability. I just wouldn't worry about that one little old bit. There is enough time to become a Sinner Boy without rushing things. I would have a little more of downstairs and a little less of upstairs if I could help it.

Now-a-days, I sit in the church house where I want to. I can be saved and safe – all at the same time and in the same spot, thank you very much. And if God sees me as a precious jewel, then I just don't have to fret myself about that part anymore. I will hear the upstairs messages but they will have to go through the basement before they get to my ears.

Getting It Right

My breath caught in my throat, my chest was tight, and my interest in personal safety increased every time we went to visit the Petrie's. Just getting there was one part of the adventure. There was this great big steep hill, probably the steepest in the whole wide world we had to go up. Dad had to put the car in low gear so we could get to the top. That hill was so steep you could drive up it if everybody held their breath so the car could make it, but it was not wise to go down it because your brakes might fail half way down. We generally went around the other way to get back home.

I have no idea how we started visiting the Petrie's. My parents were remarkable people and apparently visited up and down the streets of North Lonsdale, there in Knoxville, and one thing led to another and there we were, making family visits with the Petrie's.

His name was Mr. Petrie, and he was uncouth and mean. He must have grown up rough and lived hard, because he was all scrawny and coarse. He was a human version of a junk yard dog - mean bark, sharp teeth, and short fuse. Her name was Sister Petrie, and I never found out her other name because after she got saved she had a change of heart and name. Her mentality was different from Mr. Petrie. He yelled and she quailed. It wasn't right. I wanted to do something about it but didn't know what to do. She needed help, and I was just a kid and didn't have any useful ideas. I guess the whole family went visiting because Sister Petrie could use a little support, and then maybe Mr. Petrie could get salvation also.

The other part of the adventure was not knowing what could happen during the visit. Mr. Petrie had his ways. He was so hard on her. "Look-a her. She's a mess. Cain't keep the house. Slop all over the place." He would list her faults, which in his opinion were manifold, and all she could do was sort of choke out a chuckle constricted by acute embarrassment, "Go ahead. Tell a big-un.

227

That's a whopper. Cain't you tell a worser-un?" The reality was he could and he did. That was sort of scary to witness these interchanges, but entertaining in a nervous sort of way at the same time.

Now because she got born again in the Mennonite way, she had to reform her way of living. She needed to wear a prayer veiling all the time on account of 1 Corinthians Chapter 11. We called it a covering, and that had its own challenges for someone who didn't grow up knowing about these things. Mother knew about coverings and could put hers on just right, and it sat there like it belonged. It didn't work so smoothly for poor Sister Petrie. Her covering would twist from port to starboard, tilt fore and aft in a most unsatisfactory way. And dents, oh my goodness gracious. Her covering was dented and bashed in, sort of like the cars we saw around the place.

"Is it on right?" she would plead as we got ready to take her to church. She wanted to get it right so as not to look sloppy and to be acceptable. Mother would fix her up until things looked right.

Getting it right took about three generations of sustained teaching. Sister Petrie did not have that advantage. But, the wife of that Mennonite preacher who moved in did not get it right either, despite all the advantages. One time she wore an orange dress with little yellow flowers. Moreover, she came to the house one day without wearing her covering. "She wasn't taught right," Mother said. Mother knew about these things.

You know what? Somehow I can't help but wonder about something. Was all this energy spent on getting it right worth it? It seemed like the more I tried to get it just right, the more hopeless it got. Just couldn't get there. These days I don't worry myself about things I can't change. I will do what I can and let the rest up to God.

Sing A Song

We were such a small congregation there at 909 University Avenue - at the Knoxville Mennonite Mission. It was a small building, much smaller now than it was way back then. Things get smaller as you get older, and this is a proven fact. The outside of the Mission was made out of brick. The inside walls were hard and the ceiling was made out of tongue and groove boards. Of course the floor was hardwood as carpets was not in keeping with principles.

Back when I was growing up Mennonite in Knoxville, I did not grasp how modern we were. Acoustical engineers are employed these days to achieve the acoustical effects we had in that building, and they never get it quite right. What with all those hard surfaces, the sound bounced around like marbles going down a marble roller, and made us sound better than we were. And, not to boast, God forbid, but we were pretty good in the singing department. We did all four parts, and without musical instruments. We were just surrounded by sound, and it felt sort of like being wrapped up in a nice warm blanket.

Yes sir, we sung pretty good back then, and it was even better when these traveling groups, the Gospel Teams, from Harrisonburg or Denbigh Virginia came to town to bless and encourage us. Goodness gracious alive, how we would sing. I am sure the harmonies floated right up to Heaven and all the angels noticed and got jealous. They needed harps to stay on tune. We didn't need harps. We had each other and shape notes. Us kids learned to sing by listening and following the notes, those shape notes that told you if it was a do, re, mi, or fa and so on. Now-a days they talk about reading music. I guess none of us knew about reading music. We just sang it, and if we didn't know the song very well, we followed the shapes on the notes. Singing parts with shape notes was easy. If you couldn't get the fa later on, you would hold on the fa, humming it real lightly, until the

229

hard fa came up again. Listening to the harmony at that point made it easy to get it right, especially if the other people sang their shape right. You really ought to sing the notes right, because that is how the Mennonite Hour singers did it.

Learning from trustworthy singers made it easy to catch on. You could listen to the Mennonite Hour and learn parts by singing along, especially on that song "My God and I." They sang it in an interesting way. One verse everybody would hum but the bass voices. Then the next verse, the altos sang their part, while the humming went on. Oh, boy, that sounded good. Singing along with the tape recorder helped whenever that song came up in church.

But it was real important to use discretion when listening. Some folks didn't understand notes, shape or round. They just sang from heart, and that can lead you astray, musically speaking. The heart doesn't follow the rules or the shapes faithfully. For example, take that song, "What Can Wash Away My Sins." Folks would sing "Tha-yut makes me white as snow," with that slide upwards on the second syllable and returning to baseline on "makes." Dad, he did not approve. "Why do they have to sing THA-YUT? Why can't they sing THAT, the right way, like it is in the book?" This was a point of contention, not that it made any difference because they just went ahead and sang it the way they knew and loved.

Ignorance in these matters is one thing. Messing around with the exact notes on purpose was sort of like tampering with the Bible. Especially when people in leadership did the messing.

Now once in a while a visiting revival preacher would have us sing "Would You Be Free From Your Burden of Sin," and in that chorus, he would do unusual things. On the first verse we would sing it regular - "There is pow'r, pow'r, wonder working pow'r." Then on the second verse we went double time on pow'r: "There is pow'r pow'r, pow'r pow'r, wonder working pow'r." We got ready for verse 3 because we had an idea of what was coming next. Yup, sure enough, here it came - "There is pow-pow-pow-pow'r, pow-pow-pow-pow'r, wonder working pow'r." For verse 4, the tension was unbearable. Would he take it a step further? Well - let us say he, and some of us tried, but there are limits. We just couldn't get all those pow'rs crammed into the allotted time. Now, that was fun and entertaining, much better than stories of the End Times.

I never looked around while this was going on, but I don't recall my dad joining in to the fray of the multiple pow'rs. There was just too much power echoing around in the church house and that is not fitting. Moreover, that was not the right way to sing the song. It was frivolous, and frivolity has ramifications.

When it came to "Amazing Grace," there was no winning that battle about how it is supposed to be sung. Everybody had their own way to sing that song. Extra notes, slides, slurs, triplets, additional words, and entirely different tunes got used. Who can fight that sort of tidal wave? I heard "Amazing Grace" sung to the tune of "The House of the Rising Sun," and I am not kidding, to the tune of "Irene, Goodnight," for goodness sake.

To me, it seemed like everybody that knew anything about amazing grace sang their story their own way. They didn't worry one little bit about getting it right - they just sang and were quite content about it, which makes me wonder if working so hard to get it right makes it easier to get it wrong.

At My Expense

Expenses being what they were, we worked real hard not to incur them, and my parents did a pretty good job at that. What with the Great Depression barely over, and the economy threatening to go bust just any minute, you had to be careful about things. For example, others could buy a Brown Cow ice cream, but that cost a dime, whereas a Popsicle cost only a nickel and it had two sticks to it rather than just one, so it was a better bargain. But even that was mostly unnecessary, because one should freeze Kool-Aid in a freezer tray and make your own Popsicles. Never mind that it froze solid as ice, which it was, and never got crunchy like a Popsicle, which it wasn't. It was saving.

Yup, saving and getting saved were great virtues back when I was growing up Mennonite in Knoxville.

It had to be expensive to take a family of four children out to eat, especially because of the way we could eat. That was one thing we could do, and were encouraged, nay, compelled to do. We weren't like worldly people who were persnickety about food and didn't eat everything on their plates. So that is why we didn't go out to eat very much. It was expensive, unnecessary, and not nearly as good as Mother could make it.

Then there was this new restaurant that opened up in town, called "All You Can Eat For A Dollar." We tried it out and they had lots of food and it was good mostly. You could take a family of six, pay $6.00, and eat enough to hold you for three days. There was some saving in that, even though it took Dad's entire daily wage to feed us supper. I guess some pleasures are worth paying for, because the car would be entirely quiet on the way home as we were all full as ticks and lethargic as lions after a fantastic gorging session. Each time Mother would say, "Well, I guess they lost money on us."

I think Mother sort of enjoyed getting a bargain at someone else's expense. And as life progressed, this thought turned into a firm conviction because of personal experience.

My Grandpa Yoder would travel through Tennessee from time to time, between spells with family in Delaware and Florida. Tennessee was a more or less convenient stopping off place between Delaware and Florida, and we looked forward to those visits. I'm not sure if Grandpa did, because, once again there were four kids in a small house, and I got the impression that he was not fond of a ruckus, unless he was the one creating it. It had to be a burden to deal with a sweaty, wiggly little boy who wanted to be the center of attention, and would get in the center one way or the other.

But, on the other hand, he sort of asked for it, being as he was a good story teller. He could make anything into a story and make it sound believable and exciting. Dog stories especially. I don't think he liked dogs or cats, as he showed little affection towards our animals. He called them "Flea Bag" when that was not even their name. I didn't like that very much, but he thought it was funny, so of course it was funny. His dogs had good names, like Doc or Snyber. Snyber? Who ever heard of that name? But since it was Grandpa's dog back on the farm it had to be both a good dog and a good name for a dog, even though I thought he didn't like dogs. That is just the way it was.

And he had lots of stories about Snyber that were interesting. I sat on his lap, looking deep into his crinkly face, curious about his little bristly beard, and listening intently to the latest adventure of Snyber the dog. I was fully involved in the story, sort of in a trance state, which had to be obvious to my mother, because she said something to Grandpa in Pennsylvania Dutch. It was in Dutch because I didn't understand it. That language was reserved for secrets between my parents. And besides, things were funnier in Dutch, funnier because we couldn't understand it but the grown-ups could. What she said in Dutch was, "Bell mol vie ein Hund." I barely heard it, as I so deep in the story.

234

Grandpa understood it. What Mother said to him was, "Bark at him like a dog and scare the living daylights out of him so we can laugh and laugh and laugh at him for decades to come" and he did it. Right in the middle of the story, right in the middle of a sentence, alls-a sudden he cut loose like a yap dog that should be kicked. "Ra-Ra-Ra-Ra-Ra," he went, all five syllables rolling out in about 0.8 seconds, with his face contorted, teeth chattering and advancing upon me in a fearsome way, and his lap jiggling up and down.

Boys, I am here to tell you I nearly became undone. I tried to leap straight upward from a seated position, but my legs were too short. Besides he grabbed me at the same time. I was surrounded by sound and hands. Near as I can remember, I did not cry, nor did I wet his lap, but it had to be a close call. I suspect it was sort of funny to my Mother. And my Grandpa. Oh how they laughed. And laughed.

All that laughter at my expense and it wasn't even funny to me at the time. I was just way too shook up to appreciate the humor. Now-a-days I can sort of see the point of it all.

I guess as grim as those years were, what with the economy threatening to go bust any day now, and lots of outgo with not enough income, one had to find humor in what you could. But – why at my expense?

Company

Once in a while we were invited over to the Stoltzfus' for a meal which was a real experience. My mother was a great cook and her food tasted real good. She didn't pull any surprises on us. We knew pretty well what we would get. With Ruby, you could never tell. She was adventurous with her menus and tried out new stuff once in a while that left you wondering if this was suitable for people growing up Mennonite in Knoxville. She must have gotten recipes from magazines rather from the Mennonite Community Cookbook like she should have.

Eating at Ruby's table was pleasurable, mostly. The real problem was old Ray Stoltzfus. He had his own ideas of hospitality. I didn't like to play with him because he wouldn't let me or my brother go first like we should have because we were company. "No, I get to go first because this is my house," he would say in a meaningful tone. He was sort of unpredictable so you best take note of his tones.

Now, when the Stolztfus family came to our house to visit, the food was good and comfortable. My mother used authorized recipes and the only thing left was the decision of how good the food was. Was it normal excellent or great excellent? Mother did get adventurous with mashed potatoes by sprinkling paprika on the top and that looked so nice and inviting.

But once again, the pleasure stopped after the meal because we were supposed to play nicely with old Ray. We would try to play games with him, but they weren't good enough for him or alls-a sudden he would go first without permission. "I get to go first because I am company." Well, he was right on both counts. He was company and it was polite for him to go first. But he didn't let us feel virtuous about it – he just went first and we didn't feel good about it at all. We got mad. He took away our good intentions and we never got to go first either at his house or our own house on account of him.

Being company and having company with the Stoltzfuses was stressful, especially with that old Ray. He pushed the rules of company way too far.

But there was this one time when we had company and it wasn't the Stoltzfuses, thank goodness. This was fun company. The Greer family out there in Ohio came to visit and this was great. Our parents knew the Greers real well and were best friends with them for a long, long time. Their son was named after my dad, and my sister was named after Mrs. Greer. That is how good of friends they were. This helped a lot because the big people were relaxed and didn't talk about church problems. They talked about good times. We didn't know the Greer kids but that was OK because we could play without being nervous about tones. We had such a nice time playing on that Sunday afternoon, but like it always happens, good times come to an end. We had to change our clothes and get ready for Sunday night church.

I just knew that would happen sooner or later and it didn't seem fair. All too often going to church spoiled the fun and ruined a perfectly good day.

My brother and I knew the drill. When Mother or Dad said we were to go and get ready – well, that is what we did. "Boys" was the second reminder. We learned not to expect a third chance.

But Darrell Greer had great appreciation of good times so much so that he didn't want to change his clothes or ways. My brother and I put on our white shirts and black pants. Darrell played. His mom knocked on the door. "Darrell, are you getting ready?" He would stop playing, tug at his pants and grunt real convincing like, saying, "I can't get my pants unsnapped." After the third or fourth time, me and my brother were transfixed with admiration and horror. This was good stuff, but how long could it last?

Well, you know, all good things come to an end, for Darrell and for his mother as well. She came to the end of her patience, Darrell to the end of dallying around. "I can't get my pants unsnapped" and that bedroom door opened and shut like a shutter on a camera, open/shut, with Darrell pulled out of the room in between. We heard the sound of rapid fire swatting and cries of protest. The door opened once again, Darrell flew into the room like he was propelled by external forces, which he was, and the door shut in a firm manner.

There was evidence of trauma lingering on Darrell's cheeks. The brief time out of the room with his mother must have been instructive in pants mechanics because he announced, "I can get my pants unsnapped," and he did.

Even though we could never push the limits quite as far as that old Ray and Darrell did, we learned that it is possible to do this and survive. This was useful learning for later on in life. This is why it is good to have company on a regular basis.

I can't help it, but I often wish that I had a recording of voices of people who were important to me at various stages of life. You can sometimes find recordings of old timey music and that brings back a flood of memories of not only the songs, but also the events that are connected to them. But the sound of voices – the feel of the voice is still there, but the actual sound can get sort of dimmed over the years. There was this old song that says it all and I wish it could happen, and not only for my mother and her prayers:

If I could hear - my mother pray again.
If I could hear - her tender voice as then,
So happy I would be, it would mean so much to me
If I could hear my mother - pray again.

But we did have a device back there in Knoxville that was useful, a Bell and Howell reel-to-reel tape recorder capable of handling an 11" reel, with fast and slow speeds. What a handy tool to keep things alive, to help you remember. When there were church conferences, you could bet there would be a row of tape recorders to record the sermons.

In our house, that tape recorder got used a lot. And on occasion, sermons were played for purposes of inspiration, especially when Grandpa Yoder visited. He liked to be inspired by sermons. He had a deep desire to inspire others by sermons, but this was not to be. He had to settle for influencing others through Sunday School teaching and by various other methods.

There was this one time when he visited and listened to the tape recorder. I could tell something was going on with what he was hearing because he sat there, hunched forward, every muscle of his body tensed up to the point of quivering. At times he would stare far off into the distance and shake his head side to side, in the "No" kind of fashion, with a face that looked sort of frowny.

241

Being as it was Grandpa that could mean "Yes," that he was pleased with what he was hearing. When Grandpa was around, you needed to interpret things or you might get it wrong. Sometimes that shake of the head and the intense frown represented displeasure of the severe variety. It was hard to tell.

Kids try to learn quickly because they have a lot at stake. They want to live a little bit longer. But it was so hard to tell with Grandpa. You could see a "No" frown and believe it meant "Yes" when it really meant "No." So, it was best to assume that everything meant "No" just in case.

I sat there and observed Grandpa Yoder, waiting for further clues. Should I stay or scamper? That sideways shake of the head continued, no verbal shots were fired off, so I sort of thought the "No" look maybe might mean "Yes" this time. Then he began to make sort of moaning sounds. This was a good sign, especially when he started saying, "Eye-yi-yi." Then – it happened. He took a deep breath and I trembled. "I wish I could talk with that man," he exclaimed, then retreated to his absorption. I relaxed. It was going to be OK. Once again Grandpa moaned and repeated, "I wish I could talk with that man." That meant he approved and wanted to be in the presence of greatness.

Now, it was confusion time all over again, because he could have talked to that man right away. I knew that man's voice, every tone, and every inflection. That voice was unmistakable to me. How could I not know that voice? It was the voice of my father.

"Oh, how I wish I could talk with that man," moaned Grandpa yet once again. Being as I was young and stupid, I said, "Grandpa, you can talk to him." This was not wise. Grandpa did not appreciate comments from anybody, especially from me. He had greater appreciation for telling than being told.

Finally, I couldn't stand it any longer. "Grandpa," I said. "Go ahead and talk to him." An immediate glare for interrupting his reverie. "Go ahead because he is right there. That is my dad talking. Don't you know that?" He looked and glanced away. Dad looked and glanced away. There was this silence while the sermon continued.

This mixed me up beyond all endurance. Part of me wanted to laugh because Grandpa didn't even know he could go ahead and do what he said he wanted to do. The other part felt trembly because he didn't do what he said he wanted to do. I got all clutched up.

Grandpa wanted to talk to that man, but did not recognize the voice of his son. How could Grandpa miss it? Had that voice changed beyond recognition because of so much time and distance? How was this possible? I am sure Dad knew the voice of Grandpa. Maybe he wanted to talk to his father, and his father wanted to talk to him, but what kept it from happening? What got in the way? Maybe the Yes and No signals got mixed up. Maybe Grandpa liked the idea of talking to that man more than actually doing it. Who knows? It was too deep for a ten year-old boy to figure out.

Modern technology notwithstanding, I wonder if things between fathers and sons have changed all that much from the time when I was growing up Mennonite in Knoxville.

"If I Could Hear My Mother Pray Again," James Rowe, pub. 1922, Public Domain

Electricity

"What is electricity?" This old boy liked to ask questions that were not designed so much for answers as for discussion pieces. "You can't see it. You don't know where it comes from. You can just see the evidence of it. I think, when it comes to electricity, we are closer to the spirit world than we know."

This guy had limited formal education but was blessed with keen intelligence. He actively thought about things, and loved to figure them out. He could fix anything worth fixing and understand anything worth understanding, things both mechanical and spiritual. As a Bible believing preacher, he was a man of firm convictions with deep appreciations for clear definitions. So when it came to things electrical, he knew there were things going on beyond the physical realm on account of it being invisible yet very powerful.

Now, my dad had ideas about things as well. When we moved out to the country, Dad felt it would be a good idea to have an electric fence around the field, and I guess it was a pretty good idea, except for times when the fence needed to get fixed. And my dad liked to fix things, too. Sometimes he would fix the fence without unplugging the shocker. He would stand on a piece of wood to do his work, and make sharp grunts in a rhythmic fashion. It sounded sort of like when the old pig was sleeping next to the electric fence and I would take and drop a blade of grass on her back and then to the fence. Like dad, she wouldn't get the full impact, just enough of a tickle to be disturbing. "Wunk, wunk, wunk, wunk," she would say, right in time with the surges. As I shortened the blade of grass, it would turn into, "Wee. Wee. Wee! WEE-WEE-WEE, followed by porcine profanity. That is sort of like the sounds he would make when working on a live fence, with periodic shaking of his head and facial contortions, minus the profanity part.

But there was this one time when he yelled for Mother to turn the fencer off and she thought he said to turn it on because it was off already. She turned it on, and he grabbed ahold of the wire, and got real grouchy real quick. There was spirited conversation back and forth, but my mother thought it was sort of funny.

Electricity served as a reminder of things spiritual, like the time when Brother Ezra pronounced one Sunday that he had this feeling that someone might not be back in church the next Sunday. He didn't know why, he just had this feeling, and just in case, it would be a good idea for all of us to get right with God pretty quickly. That worried me a bit. I looked around our small congregation with sorrow, wondering who was going to get it. I for sure didn't want to be taken.

Well, it very nearly was Dad, being as he wanted to wire up something with 220 volts and didn't feel like unscrewing the fuse. He poked around with his screw driver and alls-a sudden he was looking into an arc welder, with sparks a-flying ever which-a-way, and it took the side of the screw driver right out. He was very sober the next Sunday when he told Brother Ezra that he was nearly the one who didn't make it to the next Sunday. "Well, Brother David," said Brother Ezra.

Now, even though I was young and stupid while I was growing up Mennonite in Knoxville, I didn't think that really qualified as a close call, as he should have turned the electricity off before working on it. That is what I would have done. One shouldn't mess around with live wires is what I was taught. Problem was, just because you were taught doesn't mean learned, if learning means a more or less permanent change in behavior. It was just easier to take both short cuts and your chances when it came to electricity, like when I wanted to cross the single strand electric fence. It was too low to crawl under and too high to straddle over. I didn't have a board to lift it up real careful like. So after a short time of meditation, a solution presented itself. I stood sideways to the fence, swung my left leg up and over. The intent was to push off with the right foot and swing the right leg up and over at just the right time, a straddle – hop combination.

Except I messed up somehow. Something didn't work out just right on account of the Spirit of Electricity entered my body in a most delicate location and anyone looking on would have been justified in wondering if I was a Holy Roller and had been touched. There were noises and spasmodic movements, clear evidence of something that was not seen but by gum was felt, very powerfully felt.

Boys, I got to tell you something. When you get in touch with electricity, you really are pretty close to the spirit world. And if you keep on monkeying around with either the Spirit or electricity, one of these days, you are going to pay for it. I am pretty sure that old boy would agree with me on that point.

The Laughing Dog

Some people say that animals don't have feelings. Maybe that is true with turtles. Dogs and cats show lots of feelings. I knew this on account of our cat Katrina. She got all embarrassed when my brother snuck up on her when she was all squatted down in the yard. He picked her up and then he turned around, and she peed a semi-circle like a squirt gun. We laughed like all get out, because she got this look of embarrassment on her face.

Our friends, Ralph's family, had a dog and her name was Goldie. Goldie was your basic dog with curly fur and floppy ears. I never got to know her very well, so it seemed like she was rather bland, but I am sure that wasn't totally true. Apparently she had friends in the neighborhood and she went visiting now and again so that ought to tell you something. And she must have had hospitality because other dogs would stop by for visits.

So even though I didn't get in touch with her feelings, I knew she had friendly character. After a time I started putting two and two together. After some of these visits, there was evidence of hanky-panky going on, the kind of activity we weren't allowed to do when we went visiting. On a regular basis her tummy would swell up, and then a bunch of puppies would pop out

I had to revise my opinion about her character. It seems like she kept questionable company. One of those dogs that visited Goldie was one of the happy go lucky types. He was always running around looking for what he could get into, sort of like some of the guys I knew, grinning and sticking their noses in other people's business. This old dog carried a goofy, up-to-no-good grin on his face all the time. That should be a clue.

Ralph's family didn't like that old dog hanging around anymore than Mr. Sperry appreciated me trying to hang around his daughter Patti. In East Tennessee, guns got used to make a point. And the time came when that old dog needed to understand a few things. Ralph and them had an over and under .410 shot gun/.22 rifle. A

.410 shot gun loaded with a slug could make a statement under the right circumstances. Ralph's family didn't need to resort to guns to communicate with their neighbors, even though some of them were a bit scrappy. No, they had better approaches, such as integrity and the right kind of character. But with that old opportunistic dog, diplomacy did not create a change of behavior. It just kept hanging around, causing repercussions.

When it comes to guns and dogs, you got to be careful. You better not go shooting your neighbor's dog, even if it is a mangy hateful old thing, and engages in trespassing and morally offensive behavior. You don't even talk bad about another man's dog. People there in Knox County took pride in their dogs, and it is not fitting to hurt or disparage a dog. That is when serious gun play can happen. You learn about this if you pay attention while growing up Mennonite in Knoxville.

It took a lot of wisdom to speak to that dog in a way it could understand, and in such a way as nobody found out the details. If you understand the temperament of dogs and those old boys in Tennessee, it goes a long way in deciding what to do.

Some folks don't take it amiss if they get shot. It is just a rite of passage, or a form of recreation. It gave you bragging rights. Some of them sort of laugh it off if they survive. Dogs are a little bit like that.

Considering the options, Ralph's brothers figured they could count on the essential good nature of that dog. They made preparations. There was this .410 shot gun shell they emptied out - shook all the bird shot out. Then they filled it up with rock salt, and waited until that mongrel with a happy look on his face came visiting. And there he came, trotting along just as happy as you please. He stopped by the driveway, sniffed the air, and acted like he was invited as he sauntered towards the house. He was in a good frame of mind.

One of Ralph's brothers was waiting with that gun, and just as soon as that dog made his intentions clear, that gun spoke. Say what you want, but I am pretty certain that dog didn't get mad about being thwarted. He took it all in stride, big strides. I guess he found the whole business sort of funny, because he wrinkled back his lips and burst in to laughter. "Yippee!" he screamed in laughter and surprise. "Ah hi-hi-hi-hi-yi-yow!" he exclaimed as he ran down the road. Which being interpreted meant he was thrilled to death. He was so amused he couldn't wait to get back and share the joke with his whole pack.

It was all done in a friendly sort of way, and an agreement was reached, in all civility and in proper form. That dog got a good laugh out of it, and clearly decided he might as well go pranking around somewhere else.

I may be wrong, but I think that dog was less offended than most people are when they get shot. He just took it as it was intended and dealt with it. He set an example for all of us in grinning and bearing with thwarted dreams and desires.

I Really Didn't Want to Fight

There were times I felt sorry for Bert Jefferson. I sort of got to know him from a distance at Karns High School, and it was best to know him that way. Rumor had it his old man would beat him up on a regular basis. It could have been true, but I doubt anybody knew for sure. It was not something that Bert seemed ready to talk about. Based on his general demeanor and way of dealing with disagreements, it was a real possibility that he was no stranger to violence.

Bert seemed to be a misfit, somehow. He wore clothes to school that seemed out of place - often a white shirt with long sleeves rolled half way up his arms. Those baggy gray pants did not make a fashion statement. He didn't get along too well with others because he would just as soon fight as talk. When he fought, it was mean and dirty. When he talked, it was mean and dirty. The best I ever heard out of him was when he would hoot at you like a howling monkey, with his little mouth shaped in a hard little circle: "Ah hoo, hoo, HOO." That meant you better get out of there pretty quick.

Now when it came to fighting, I knew I wasn't supposed to. It wasn't allowed because the Bible said so. Being as I grew up Mennonite in Knoxville, we were supposed to get used to suffering, shame, and not resisting evil, because that is the way Jesus wanted it to be. No fighting no matter what, no matter who started it, no matter the cost.

Basically all the preachers there in Knox County said they believed in the Bible, every single word of it, and that you were supposed to listen up the best you could. But what they said left a lot of wiggle room for them. They had ways of making exceptions in these kinds of circumstances. They preached dispensation. That meant you could dispense with some of those impossible rules the Mennonites believed in because it didn't apply exactly to this day and time. It was an idea of how things might work out some other time way off in the future.

Now, I learned that whatever Jesus said was the gospel truth and you were supposed do it, or not do it, depending on the situation. We believed that anything Jesus said applied right now except for the part about cutting off your hands or gouging out your eyes. We could dispense with that part.

That No Fighting rule got deeply implanted. That rule made life pretty rough for me. I never got to settle things the manly way, like thrashing it out and getting it over with. Seemed like that was a good way to clear the air and gain some prestige. You gained prestige by combat wounds, like getting a tooth knocked out. Then you could show it off by pulling your lip back and saying, "Look-a that. He knocked that tooth right out of my head." Another way was to strut around like a banty rooster, and relying on your friends to hold you back. Then you could say, "I would of tore his head right off. I would of kilt him. It took six guys to hold me back."

Of course there would be a big audience whenever a fight broke out. Mostly it was verbal assaults and air boxing, and maybe some dust raising unless somebody backed down. Backing down was a shameful thing to do, because you were nothing in the eyes of everybody in the whole school for not getting beat up.

Old Bert wasn't bogged down by those rules. He didn't need a lot of provocation to start a real fight. I tried real hard to stay out of his way, to escape his notice. I was pretty low in the pecking order which meant I needed to be careful. No point in getting into a situation that called for fighting because I wasn't supposed to and I didn't know how to. So I didn't need any more humiliation in my life. That is why I sort of crept around.

There was this one time that I said something to Bert and he figured I needed to be straightened out. He began to prance around, yelling, "You want to fight, huh? Come on, you want to fight, huh?" Within ten seconds there were around 50 kids in circle around us yelling "Fight! Fight!"

I really didn't want to fight nobody, especially Bert Jeffries. But it seemed like I ought to because everybody expected it out of me. I couldn't be a chicken and not take him on, even if I would have been beat up real bad. What an awful quandary because of theology and cowardice. There was no glorious way out. For me, there would have been no glory, no pride in battle wounds. Nothing but another castor oil dose of humiliation. Jesus' words about the blessings of loving your enemy added shame to humiliation because I wasn't doing real good with that commandment.

So I just stood there, arms hanging by my side, tail scrunched between my legs, wondering if my yellow belly was glowing like a neon light.. "Well, ain't ye gonna fight or what, huh?" yelled Bert. "Don't ye want to fight, huh? Come awn. Ye-a chicken, huh?" while he bounced around, kicking up dust and ready to make me have to turn the other cheek. "Nah, I ain't gonna fight you" I choked out and disappointed that great crowd of witnesses to my chickenhood. Dripping with shame, I shouldered my way out of the circle, knowing that I was now reduced to less than nothing in the social order.

It just wasn't fair that theology stunted my social development. Absolutely nobody gave me a kind word of understanding about what I had to deal with. Bert got that from the popular girls. Some of the guys were talking about Bert, kind of making fun of him because he was sort of uncivilized and how his old man would beat him. "Aw," said one of the popular girls. "He has had a rough life." Everybody got respectful of Bert at that moment.

That nearly caused me to choke on my own fury. So what if he had a rough life? What about me? At that moment, I didn't feel sorry for him no more. I thought I had sort of a rough life too, but nobody noticed that part at all.

I bet if I would have been a bit more of a bad boy and believed in dispensation, I could have had a chance at acceptance. But I wasn't brave enough to be bad or good enough to get popular.

It took a bit of time, like several decades, until I found a way to get over it. I can't help but wonder – Did it have to be that way?

I Should Of Known Better

Since it is such a sensitive topic, I never asked my brother or sisters about it, but I know how it was for me. I know for a fact that I wet the bed, longer than I should have. Whether this was related in any way to being called Kenny or growing up Mennonite in Knoxville, or a combination of the two I don't know for sure. Like I say, I don't have comparative data. It just doesn't do to go around asking people who grew up Mennonite in Knoxville if they wet the bed. But I did, and got called Kenny, so there could be a connection somehow.

Mother had sense of humor, I guess you could say, for things she felt were funny, especially when I didn't see it that way at all. "Kenny wet the bed?" she would ask and I would protest with all the outrage I could muster up, and that created hilarity. The proof of this is those reel-to-reel tape recordings that would get sent back and forth to Grandpa Schlabach containing family news, us children singing, and so forth. Right there it is: "Kenny wet the bed?" and me going "UnnnaaaAAAHH!"

Grandpa Schlabach had a similar sense of humor because he sent that selfsame tape back and added his commentary right after I made my noise. With his monotone, nasal, and ponderous voice he recorded: "So, Kenny wet the bed, huh?"

Now, was all that necessary? They say bed wetting is somewhat normal for little kids, right? Or else why do they have diapers and pampers and so forth? I didn't know any better – that is was what it was.

When I got to more of a verbal stage of development, I came up with a defense mechanism. Like humans at all places and all times, I placed the responsibility on someone more vulnerable. It wasn't me that wet the bed at all. I explained that some old colored woman crawled into my bed and wet the bed. Now where did that come from? I don't know where it came from, but when it came out, it created more opportunities for marveling at the cuteness of Kenny.

257

I now know that it wasn't anybody else in my bed. It was just your regular lapse of bladder control, and a wish to avoid the embarrassment of it all, and I wished it so hard that it became true in my mind. I also know now that it was, maybe is still, regular practice to blame all sorts of ills on people of color.

I didn't know any better. I was just a kid acting like a kid growing up where racial equality was not the radar screen of social awareness. So, such comments coming out of the mouth of a more or less innocent child were cute.

As time went on, I finally got over the bed wetting, but the fear of an unplanned event lingered for a while.

I wish it was a more complete picture of innocence to other episodes of childhood behavior, especially when it came to scapegoating. It had to do with a game that someone invented, and we thought it was funny. It used a hateful word, the N- word, over and over again. It is such a hateful word I won't even spell it out.

The game was called "Old N- Mammy," and it involved a troupe of children. "It" would hobble down the side walk, and the rest of us would follow, chanting "Old N- Mammy," in that sing-song way like when children sing out "Nanny nanny poo poo." "It" would turn around and demand, "Who sent you?" One of us would reply, "Yo' uncle," or some such relation. "It" would turn around, and the same thing kept on going, until the response was "Yo' Mamma." Upon which "It" would chase us down the street, catch some body, then the new "It" could lead the pack.

It was so much fun to drag out the tension, and the somewhat marginal awareness that what we were singing out was not exactly proper. There was a wicked thrill in doing something our parents didn't know about. So, just how innocent was it?

There is embarrassment about wetting the bed, and being blessed with reminders about it. There is puzzlement about blaming it on the old colored woman. Worse yet is that stupid old game.

Since it is sort of a sensitive issue, I never asked my brother and my sisters if they knew about this game, or if they ever played it. For me, I should have known better, and I guess I sort of did, but it didn't change anything very much. I was a joyful and willing participant and for that I am ashamed.

Accidental Lesson

Back when I was 15 years old and growing up Mennonite in Knoxville, I more or less made a decision to attend that Mennonite High School up in The County, otherwise known as Lancaster County, Pennsylvania. Not exactly sure why my mind turned that direction. Maybe I was tired of living in Knoxville and dealing with the discomfort of being the odd man out there at Karns High School.

Being as it was a Mennonite School I reckoned it would be a Christian school and things would be different there. I needed something different being as I was weary of being different in Knox County and figured on all of us being different in the same way up in The County. It wouldn't be so awkward anymore. I also heard it was a good school and you get a good education there.

I guess you can say I had great expectations.

But being there was different than I thought. I guess when you are different, you are different no matter where you are. The County and That School were not well adapted for a person such as me. They talked different. They acted different. They thought different. I couldn't figure it out. I knew I was still different and still felt awkward.

They had a dean at That School as well as a principal. That was different. In Tennessee we didn't have a dean. We had a principal, he was in charge, and that was that. Didn't know what a dean was or what he was supposed to do. Knew what a principal was, but didn't know what he was supposed to do there. Maybe the both of them didn't know either.

There were these rules we were supposed to follow whether we wanted to or not because of The Discipline of The Conference in The County. The Dean seemed to be the one that signed the papers if you did something wrong and needed to get it right again.

Some students had lots of lessons in doing better, with lots of those neat signatures of The Dean on the

261

papers. He had neat hand writing, and wrote in a straight line, except it wasn't parallel to straight. It angled up to the right, which was an indication of his leanings.

There were a lot of mighty right Mennonites in The County back in those days. Far as I know there still is that kind around, pretty much the same only a little different.

The Dean would let us know publicly about expectations. He would say, "Ve are not ea-guh..." and the rest would follow and a wise person understood the code talk. I guess I understood enough, but I wasn't eager to learn a whole lot about what he wasn't eager to have happen. So many things he was not so eager about.

One student got caught in a tropical downpour and needed to get from one building to another. The rain made her late, and she needed to get a permission slip from The Dean. To justify her lateness, she wrote, "It takes longer to swim than to walk." He was not eager to accept that in the spirit it was given.

Another guy watched a teacher fill up his car from the teachers' gas pump on campus. The teacher, they called him Eggum on account of his initials, didn't pay attention and spilled gas. This guy called out something like "Where I come from, we put the gas in the tank." Well. They weren't eager to deal with that situation. In fact, they weren't eager so much that they cast him out of the school.

So they weren't eager to accept a lot of stuff. What about me? Me vassn't so eager to deal with their eagerness or lack thereof and far as I could tell that didn't make any difference. Come to think of it, The Dean's eagerness didn't make much of a dint in my behavior. I guess there were some things that even he couldn't change and he just had to deal with it.

Maybe that was the best lesson I learned there, quite unintended and by accident. It wasn't part of the curriculum and I didn't get a grade on it. In a word, just because you aren't eager to deal with something doesn't necessarily mean a thing. It will happen anyway, and all you can do is deal with it the best you can.

Oh Yeah

Once in a while I get accused of making things up. Just because I tell a good story now and again they say I am storying. Well, I got to tell you something. Sometimes the story is truer than the event itself. The bare bones facts are as interesting as a column of fractions you are supposed to add up. And furthermore, if you are good at it, you don't even have to experience something to remember it.

Lots of stories surrounded me while I was growing up Mennonite in Knoxville, and most of them were actually helpful. I never bothered myself about the facts of the matter - a well told story helped me learn stuff, like you best not be messing with another man's wife because it can lead to misunderstandings.

It went like this - Brother Ezra operated a rolling store there in Kentucky before he came to Knoxville. He was a preacher there also. He got friendly with all his customers and was helpful whenever he could be. Take like the time this woman needed a ride to get to the doctors or something. He helped out and her old man got mad about it, being as he thought it was improper. He came over to the house and threatened to "cut off ye head and th'ow it down the mountain." Even though it didn't happen to me, it felt real, like it could have been my head rolling down the mountain side.

Back in the day my dad was full of stories of when he was growing up and when he lived in Virginia. I used to live in Virginia also being as I was born there in the farmhouse in McGaheyesville, but I don't remember a thing of it on my own. But I know about it. I heard the stories about stuff, about the fish that got washed up in a hole in the creek and how it stayed there until it grew up and made a fish supper, and the times my brother was so afraid the car would back down in a hole, and the little Crosley that was so underpowered it could hardly make it

265

up the hill. It moved so slow Dad could get outside and keep up with it by walking.

I thought they were pretty good stories until one day my little sister chimed in. She was always poking her nose into stuff and being treated nice because she was the littlest, which she was. She was such a pain that I needed to bring balance to her life by being mean to her. And when that story about the Crosley came up, she said with the enthusiasm of a shared experience, "Oh Yeah," clearly meaning she was there and she remembered it.

Now that was just too much. That story happened in Virginia and she wasn't even born yet. For Pete's sake. And besides I heard the story first and for a fact knew she wasn't there, so why did she have go and act like she knew all about it when she didn't know nothing about it?

It was beyond all endurance and I am sure I helped her understand that best I could. Now let me be clear. I am not making anything up here. I don't know what happened next, except I didn't forgive her for putting on, and based on history there may have been some ramifications for me. I was just young and stupid at the time.

But you know what? It didn't matter one single solitary bit if she was there or not. Because in a way of speaking she was there being as it was a family story and she was part of the family even though I wasn't in favor of that and being family means you have a common history whether you were actually there or not.

"You remember that Crosley?" Well, I did - not in the way of remembering it by riding in it, seeing it, seeing Dad walk beside it and all. I did see a picture of it and the rest was up to me. I remembered the stories, so yeah, I remembered the Crosley.

But for my little sister to act like she remembered it - that was not truthful. She was storying. I could not allow that, and besides I claimed that story. She was an intruder in the family far as I was concerned so how could she up and remember something like that?

I guess I was afraid of being less of a member of

the family if she started remembering the same stories.

Oh Ken, Ken, Ken. For shame. I didn't get the truth about remembering, and created a lot of pain for nothing. Oh yeah, and that is the truth.

Tell Him I Said Hidey

We knew him as Brother Sol. He had a last name, but it didn't get used much. Sol was probably short for Solomon, but I didn't know that for sure. He was an old man, very old, probably sixty or something. And he was a fixture there at the Concord Mennonite Church, a faithful member.

I knew him as Brother Sol, but I am not sure how he knew me. He came off and on to Ball Camp Elementary School when they needed a maintenance guy and it was good to see someone I knew from church. Didn't want to be a pest, but wanted to be friendly-like, and I would walk over to the trunk of his ancient car while he looked for tools in the trunk, and say "Hello Brother Sol," very quietly because I didn't want others to hear the Brother part. They wouldn't understand. It is somewhat doubtful if he actually knew me because he would say, "Hey, boy." Then I would saunter away, having done my job of connecting with a fellow church member.

My friend Ralph, who helped me by example to stay somewhat on the path of righteousness, was very observant of behavior, and knew Brother Sol much better than I. Ralph told me to watch Brother Sol in church one Sunday when the flies were about. This one pesky fly landed on the top of his right ear, danced a jig, and then flew away for a season. Brother Sol, being delayed of reaction, swished his ear long after that fly was out of the danger zone. That was welcome diversion for us during church time.

I could do my own observation as well. Being as Brother Sol was the regular song leader, and I enjoyed singing, I watched how he did things. While remaining seated in the seat, he announced the hymn number in a clear voice, and then thumped on something and held it up to his ear. After humming around lightly for a bit, he started the song with his strong voice. Once in a while he invited us to select a hymn. You needed to be quick - "Any sh-lechuns - if not, number - "

After serious observation, I came to a conclusion he was getting the pitch from that object which was called a tuning fork. The remaining puzzle was how he got the right pitch as the songs had all kinds of sharps and flats and that made some sort of a difference, somehow. But he knew how to work things so it came out exactly right.

Not only could he fix things at schools there in Knox County and lead singing at church at the Concord Church, he could remember old people. Some of them were still alive, and lots of them weren't anymore. Every once in a while we needed to know who was buried in the cemetery to fill in the blank places on the cemetery map. Brother Sol would know.

My soon-to-be brother-in-law used to live out there at Concord along Dutchtown Road a long, long time ago and he came a-visiting one time. He knew Brother Sol. Brother Sol couldn't quite place him until mention he was Harry's son.

Brother Sol's face lit up with the pleasure of remembrance. With the only display of emotion I ever witnessed from him, said: "Oh, so you're Harry's boy? Well, when you see him, you tell him I said hidey." He wanted to be remembered to Harry being as he had positive memories of their time together, best as I could tell.

Oh, Brother Sol. You have long since passed over to the other side since when I was growing up Mennonite in Knoxville. How many other saints are with you now in Glory Land? If you can hear me, I ask you, if you see Brother Ezra, Ruth Byler, Brother Jennings, and all them - if you see them, tell them I said hidey and that I miss them a whole lot.

I suppose mothers everywhere have a way of making their meanings clear without using a lot of words. That certainly was the case back in the day. Sometimes just a look, a clearing of the throat, a clenched jaw, or a single word.

"Supper." That meant you better wash your hands, get in a good mood, and get to the table without having to make Dad wait. Being as he was the daddy he had the privilege of being the last one to the table and we had the honor of waiting on him.

"Davit." That meant that Dad his own self was pushing the limit and the food was going to get cold and it wasn't going to get cold. Period. Now he couldn't see the distant gaze and the pulsing jaw muscle but I am sure he could hear it, because David rarely lingered after that summons.

It was sort of a code, once in a while the code was unmistakable in meaning. Sometimes new words got invented and even I could understand what it meant, mostly. Years after I got done growing up Mennonite in Knoxville I discovered science had studied these things, and figured out only 7% of the meaning of communication came through the words. My experience and scientific findings come pretty close to the same conclusion. You got to pay attention to meaning beyond the words so as to get the point.

Mother could make her point, very clear indeed, when the need arose. Take for instance, when I was especially unkind to my little sister, and verbal admonishment did not yield desired behavior, Mother would just walk to the pantry, open the door, get that wore out, brown belt without a buckle off the nail, and just lay it down on the table. That act demanded attention and the meaning was clear, especially when I was acting all dense and everything. That belt was worn to a frazzle and was very supple and spoke with authority. Don't ask me how I know. We will just let that part alone, with a

271

parting comment about me being a fast learner on some things. Not fast on learning to be kind but quick to learn about the consequences if you aren't. It hurt, and it still hurts to think about it. I didn't like it, and I don't like pantries.

Belts and pantries created pain on several levels, just like lots of things can and do, if you stop and think about it.

I got to thinking about this one time that my brother did something by accident and I got hurt. Well sir. I was hurt and offended. There was pain and there was the deep offense he created and he needed to know the full extent of my agony without code words. On my part, at that time, I didn't believe in the 7% rule. The more words the better. The volume, tone, facial expressions, bodily contortions just added a bit of drama. It helped out a little bit in expressing my outrage.

My brother, being the honorable child he was, immediately expressed his remorse at the accident, which he did not mean to do. "I am sorry," he said. Me, being who I was, was not in a frame of mind to hear those words. I had some suffering to do, and the scales needed to be balanced. If I was in pain, then somebody else better be hurting too. "But, I *said* I am sorry," my brother tried again.

Sorry? What you talking about, boy? You want sorry, just you wait and we will see who is sorry. I wasn't done yet. In the most anguished style I could create, I bellowed, "But it still hurts!"

I guess you can say that wasn't very generous or forgiving on my part.

Such a racket brought Mother on the scene. It seems Mother was always popping up at the most inopportune times. She heard "I am sorry," and she heard "But it still hurts."

"Na-at," said Mother.

It was sort of like catching a glimpse of heaven there at 1018 Connecticut Avenue, being as there were no more tears and all was peaceful. When Mother spoke in code by saying "Na-at," things became clear. All manner of things. I understood what she meant. It meant things like stop that right now. Keep on going and I will give you something to cry about. Don't make me have to get out that belt. Your brother said he was sorry so this thing is over with. If you don't accept his apology, there will be some character reformation going on. Watch it buster, you are pushing the limits real bad and are on the way across the line and you better not go there. I will fix it so you won't die but you will think you are, and it won't bother me too much at all. You better remember if you don't forgive your brother, God won't get around to forgiving you.

Like I said, all that from "Nat."

Well, sir. I got to tell you something. If somebody hurts you, you better believe it hurts. And you best get on with the business of forgiving even though it still hurts or else bad things will happen to you.

I don't know why some animals act the way they do. Their behavior is downright shameful, immoral, and embarrassing to think about. Why do dogs do what dogs do when they meet each other? You might think that cats are peaceful, but that is not entirely correct. Just let a strange cat come around and even a Mennonite cat will act as if it never once got saved. I just don't get it.

Then there are these birds that take advantage of others, for instance those cowbirds. They aren't much to look at and have little sense of social responsibility. They mess around, get their eggs fertilized, and then take and lay their eggs in another bird's nest since they don't make nests of their own. That baby cowbird grows big and fast, and crowds the others out of the nest and demands way too much attention from the fake parents. Altogether, cowbirds are not good examples.

Now back when I was growing up Mennonite in Knoxville, I am sure that I demanded way too much attention and probably sucked most of the air out of the room more than once. My poor mother. She had her hands full with a son that didn't know how to be anything else than what he was, no matter how hard he tried, at least some of the time. Thinking it over, I am sure there were good reasons for my mother to say, "You aren't one of mine. Some cowbird laid an egg in my nest." That was a very creative observation, and was always said with that crooked grin she had when she had to deal with things. I never thought much about it or took it too personal, except I did wonder if I was adopted from the pound somewhere being as I was so out of step and all, and it did raise a question now and again about who I belonged to – my mother or that stupid cowbird.

She was my mother and I was her son. That is a fact. No cowbird could take that away from either of us. We were sort of stuck with each other, and it wasn't such a bad arrangement when you get down and really think about it.

When I got to college I learned about Maslow's hierarchy of needs and stuff, and how a basic human need is to belong. Shoot. That wasn't such a brilliant observation. I could of wrote that, being as I knew all about it my own self, and gotten rich and famous like he did.

In fact, I learned about it in a very powerful way, not so very long ago when I started connecting with my aunt, Miz Naomi. She is a very special person, and the world is a better place because of her. She has known her cup of sorrow, and claimed a larger portion of joy. She is an inspiration to her children, grandchildren; in fact, she inspires everyone around her to be more of who they can be. She isn't Catholic or anything like that, and she would deny it, but in my book she is a saint. Not an unearthly saint, but a real person who knows and loves Jesus, and can't help but pass along goodness to everybody she meets.

She won a huge place in my heart during one of our phone calls. I told her how much I love her. "Well," she said, "you are one of mine." Evertime I talk to her, she asks, "How are you doing, my boy?" I tell you what. I can hear, feel, and see her lovely face crinkled with life and wisdom, her warm voice brimming with love, and it just oozes all over me and runs down into the cracks of my being and fills up empty spaces. She said I am one of hers. She calls me "my boy." Now that is big stuff.

Well, you sort of expect your parents to speak the same words, but it is somehow different when somebody says those words when they don't have to. Miz Naomi doesn't exactly have to say them, but she wants to and so she does.

My mother has long passed over to Glory, and one of these days it will be Miz Naomi's turn. Somehow I have this feeling that Jesus stands there by the gates and will say the same thing to Miz Naomi as he said to my mother. I just know it. Don't ask me how I know it, because I won't tell you, being as I don't know how I know it – but Jesus will look at Miz Naomi and say, "Welcome, my daughter. You are one of mine."

And I have a sneaking suspicion that when it is my time, Mother will grin and Miz Naomi will beam as Jesus takes a good look at me and say, "Well, for a son of a cowbird you done pretty good. That don't matter none, my boy, because you are one of mine."

AFTERWORD

Ken Ain't in Knoxville No More

Now let me explain something right off the bat. I know for a fact, certain and sure, that I grew up Mennonite in Knoxville. Lots of people don't think that has anything to do with anything, and that it don't necessarily mean a thing. I tried and tried to explain how it worked back in the day, but they still don't get it. Worse yet, they just outright disbelieve when I tell them. Some of those miserable reprobates took and formed the *Ken Don't Know Nothing And He Exaggerates It Anyhow Club* and take pride in their basic ignorance. That used to make me just boil with indignation, but it don't work on me that way anymore. I just pity them. They have poverty of experience and imagination, both of which you got to have if you want to survive during and thrive after growing up the way I did.

And besides, I never ever once said that my words are infallible, or verbally and plenary inspired like the Word of God. Facts is either too boring or too wild to stick to them exactly as they happened. You got to deal with stuff, and the best way of doing it is to handle it in a way so as to make sense. That calls for going for meaning, and using the facts to support it. It isn't storying any more than the Bible does. You take the Bible, now. It goes for messages eternal. Those guys that wrote it would talk about ax heads floating on water, bears eating up kids on account of them teasing a prophet on account of his bald head, a talking donkey, and riding around in chariots of fire.

Well, I got to admit here that I am not sure what the underlying eternal message of those stories is, exactly. I am pretty sure that we will find out about it over there in Glory Land. And furthermore, I am sure those guys didn't worry about every single solitary little detail, and neither do I. They told their story in a way to get you to snap to attention, listen up, and ponder stuff. That is the way of me. I tell it, and don't exactly know what it means, and you can ponder on it if you want to. Don't have to, far as I am concerned. Just don't give me no grief about each little figment. You are messing with stuff you don't get, and are picking on stuff that causes aggravation.

Go on ahead. You will be sorry one day when Jesus comes. I'm not saying anything. I am just saying.

Like I was saying, I was there. Another fact is that I am not there anymore, and that is partly good and partly not so good. The good part is that I got a good dose of nostalgia, and that is sustaining when things get rough. And I got interesting experiences that most other folks didn't and I am proud of that. The not so good part we can leave alone for right now.

Back when I was 18 or so, I left Knoxville for good and went on my way that wound around this-a way and that-a way and here I am now. Collecting stuff here and there, shedding stuff all over the place like a snake skin. People say you can take the boy out of the country but you can't take the country out of the boy, and that is supposed to be a deep thought. It isn't. It is just the way it is and the way it ought to be.

You see, in a way, I was growing up Mennonite in Knoxville long before I existed. As far back as I can remember and beyond, my father and his father and his father's father and so on were of Mennonites or Amish persuasion whether they wanted to be or not, and were sort of uncomfortable with that fact and with the geography where they were. My Grandpa Yoder wound up in Delaware and he fought the land and his religion with an intensity that nearly ruined him, but he couldn't get shed of either one. He just stayed in a tizzy all his live long life. He said he would have crawled on his hands and knees if it would get him out of Delaware, even though I don't know where he would have crawled to for some satisfaction. Besides I am not sure he could have either gotten away or found satisfaction given the nature of things. He never quite got over it. So I got a good dose of it through my family generics.

And, when you grow up living like as if you were in the bottom right hand corner of the morgue, well, that sort of influences things. When I went to college and all, I learned about nature and nurture and how they add one to another. Heck, they got it wrong. They multiply and make your life bigger than by addition. They stick around like grease on your hands. You can take and scrub with a scrub brush and that doesn't make it go away – it just gets deeper in your skin and sort of stays there until you grow some new skin if you are lucky, and if you are really lucky, some of it stays anyhows.

And that is sort of the way it is with me. I am not there anymore. But it sort of stuck like grease on my hands, and that isn't such a bad thing after all. I kind of like having greasy hands now and again in these foreign parts where I abide on account of some stuff slips off and won't take, and when I get in some situations, it helps me to slide along just fine.

You take like when I was out in Armpit, Arkansas doing a training for some folks out there. I got to talking about things that can go from bad to worse if you don't work at it. I said it could go worser and worser. Well now, that communicated what I was trying to say. They understood. And I said that in fact, it will get even more worser. "Now you are talking our language," they said, right out loud. They knew. They understood. I don't know if they grew up in a mortuary, but they still got what I was trying to say. Even though we didn't spend time discussing it directly, those folks went to church even of a Wednesday evening, and knew about getting saved and all. I am pretty sure they knew about complimenting menfolks by admiring their dogs. They knew how to talk and stuff. I felt right at home there on all accounts. Oh yeah.

So, OK. I grew up Mennonite in Knoxville. And it still sticks. And if that bothers you, get over it. I did. It don't make me no difference how you feel about it or if you don't like how I tell it. See, I got the advantage because I am a better man on account of it all.

Made in the USA
Lexington, KY
24 April 2017